THE ULTIMATE HISTORY OF
ASTON MARTIN

Marks and Spencer p.l.c.
Baker Street, London W1U 8EP
www.marksandspencer.com

A copy of the CIP data for this book is available from the British Library upon request.

The rights of Andrew Noakes to be identified as the author of this work have been asserted in accordance with Section 77 of the Copyright, Designs and Patents Act of 1988.

Created, designed, produced and packaged by Stonecastle Graphics Ltd

Designed by Paul Turner and Sue Pressley
Edited by Philip de Ste. Croix

Printed and bound in China

ISBN: 1-84273-963-8

Photographic credits.

The Aston Martin Heritage Trust: pages 10 (br), 14(tl), 24(t), 26(t), 27, 32(t), 58(t), 188
Stephen Golby: page 94
The GP Library: pages 44(t), 46(t), 50(t), 53(b), 54, 59(b), 63, 66(b), 131, 132, 134, 135, 136(t)
The Geoffrey Goddard Collection: page 48(br)
Malcolm Green: page 115
David Hawtin: page 13
Philip Jones: pages 14(tr), 77(b), 150(b)
Trevor Legate: page 83(b)
The Motoring picture Library, Beaulieu: page 43(b)
Roger Stowers: pages 12(tl), 14(bl), 14(br), 15(tr), 21(bl), 31, 40, 42(b), 64(b), 78(b), 79(t), 79(br), 92(t), 92(b), 93, 95(t), 95(br), 97(b), 98(tr), 98(bl), 99, 100, 101, 102, 106(t), 107(b), 119(b), 144(tl), 186, 187

Other pictures © Neill Bruce's Automobile Photolibrary by:
Geoffrey Goddard: pages 18(bl), 18(br), 19(b), 45(tr), 47, 48(l), 65(b), 104, 106(b), 107(t), 108, 109, 110, 111, 112(l), 117, 121(t), 128, 129, 130
Christian Gonzenbach: Pages 161(b), 162(t), 170, 172(tr), 173(t)
Beng Holm: page 140
Stefan Lüscher: page 154(br)

All other photographs © Neill Bruce's Automobile Photolibrary, with the exception of the following, which are manufacturer's press pictures supplied from The Peter Roberts Collection c/o Neill Bruce: pages: 6, 10(tl), 10(bl), 11(t), 12(tr), 42(t), 46(b), 55, 82, 97(t), 118(b), 126(t), 133(bl), 149, 151, 154(t), 154(bl), 155, 156(cl), 156(b), 157, 158, 160(cl), 161(t), 162(b), 163, 164, 165, 166, 168, 169, 171, 172(tl), 173(b), 174, 175, 176, 177, 178, 179, 183(t), 189, 190, 191, 192

All picture research by Neill Bruce, who would like to thank Neil Murray of the Aston Martin Heritage Trust for his great help in researching many of the historic pictures.

Special thanks to Roger Stowers – Aston Martin's historian and archivist – for all his advice and help with pictures, some of which have never before been published.

Also, thanks to Philip Jones of Byron International, Nigel Dawes and Duncan Hamilton Ltd. and all the owners for making available many of the cars. The 15/98 saloon and Atom were photographed by kind permission of the Birmingham Botanical Gardens.

As *The Ultimate History of Aston Martin* went to press the sudden and sad death of Victor Gauntlett was announced. As chairman of Aston Martin in the 1980s, Victor Gauntlett revitalized the company and returned it to motor racing, and Aston enthusiasts everywhere will mourn his passing.

MARKS &
SPENCER

THE ULTIMATE HISTORY OF
ASTON MARTIN

ANDREW NOAKES

Above 1996 DB7 Volante.

Contents

Above *Vanquish in action.*

Introduction

Lionel Martin first linked his own name with that of a well-known hillclimb to create 'Aston Martin' in 1914. He could scarcely have believed that 90 years later the marque would be one of the most revered sports car makers in the world. Nor could he have known that Aston Martin would build a reputation as the connoisseur's supercar, the World Champion racing car, the Englishman's Ferrari, and the car of choice for enthusiasts ranging from the Prince of Wales to James Bond. It has become all of these things, and more.

The Ultimate History of Aston Martin tells the unique story of this fascinating marque. It traces the development of Lionel Martin's early racing machines into exclusive road cars and, once Martin himself had moved on, the emergence of successful sporting cars built under the guidance of A.C. Bertelli. From there, it leads us to the advanced pre-war Atom prototype which so capably demonstrated Aston Martin's potential and convinced industrialist David Brown to save the company in 1947. *The Ultimate History of Aston Martin* chronicles the achievements of the DB era – blending the best of Aston Martin and another DB purchase, Lagonda, into a world-famous line of cars, and winning a World Championship for Britain on the track – but it also describes the shadow that fell over the whole company when, finally, David Brown relinquished control in 1972.

The story of the 1970s was one of takeovers and bankruptcy, but it also witnessed the emergence of a generation of accomplished V8 Aston Martins which would build on the company's already formidable reputation. It would see Aston Martin return, briefly, to the scene of its greatest triumph on the track – at Le Mans – and develop such audacious and controversial cars as the striking, wedge-shaped Lagonda saloon and the gullwing-doored 'Bulldog' prototype. The 1980s saw the company dragged back from the edge of extinction – again – and then slowly built into a profitable car maker. Finally it achieved a firm financial footing thanks to investment from automotive giant Ford. That gave Aston Martin the chance to invest in new models – not just replacements for the venerable V8 cars, but a whole new class of Aston Martin, bringing with it the return of the famous 'DB' name.

Astons have always blended traditional skills, using quality materials, with the best of modern technology, and the launch of the Vanquish in 2001 proved that there is still a place for both philosophies in a modern Aston Martin. Under the skin lies a Cosworth-developed V12 engine, a Formula One-style paddle-shift gearbox and an innovative structure combining carbon fibre and extruded aluminium alloy. But that Ian Callum-styled aluminium skin blends modern ideas with styling cues from one of Aston Martin's most distinctive models, the DB4GT Zagato of the 1960s. The Vanquish – and the more recent announcement of the Zagato-styled DB AR1 'American Roadster' – shows Aston Martin can take on anything from the German or Italian supercar manufacturers, and do it without forgetting the 90-year story that lies behind the famous winged emblem. This is that story.

The Early Years

Above Robert Bamford.

Above Lionel Martin.

Right Lionel Martin in 'Coal Scuttle', the first Aston Martin, at Nailsworth Ladder.

Like many other famous marques, Aston Martin's story begins with a company selling and servicing other manufacturer's cars. Just before the First World War, Robert Bamford and Lionel Martin ran a repair garage in Chelsea in West London, with an agency for Singers. In 1912, when Bamford and Martin first formed a partnership, a new Singer Ten had been introduced, and it proved to be a popular small car. In addition to servicing and repairing them, Bamford and Martin started to modify the Singers for use in trials, hillclimbs and races, with some success. But by 1914 Martin wanted to go a step further. Rather than compete using modified Singers, he wanted to build his own car.

This was intended to be a fast touring car, also capable of competition use, with the emphasis firmly on quality. It was to be built for what Martin described as the 'discerning owner driver'. The engine for the new car was a side-valve Coventry Simplex unit with a 66.5mm bore and 100mm stroke, giving a capacity of 1389cc, and this was initially installed in a 1908 Isotta Fraschini chassis to act as a test bed while other parts for the new car were being made. The new car was officially announced in October as an 'Aston-Martin', linking Martin's name with that of Aston Hill, the famous hillclimb near Aylesbury in Buckinghamshire. Nicknamed 'Coal Scuttle' – apparently a reference to the shape of the car's body – this first car clocked up 15,000 miles (24,100km) during the war, both on the road and in competition.

War prevented the construction of a second car until 1920. Initially this was fitted with the 1389cc engine, but in 1921 a heavily revised engine appeared. Though still a side-valve unit with integral head and block, the new engine boasted a third main bearing, better lubrication, and a 107mm stroke expanding the capacity to 1486cc, making the car still more competitive in the 1½-litre racing class. In this form it was road-tested by the British motoring weeklies *The Motor* (in May) and *The Autocar* (in October), achieving a 72mph (116km/h) top speed.

Previous page 1933 Aston Martin Le Mans 2/4.

Breaking records

Around this time Bamford resigned, Martin brought in his wife Katherine as a director, and the company moved to new, larger premises a couple of miles away in Abingdon Road, Kensington. Prices were announced for production models, which were essentially the same as the 1920 prototype, but with the addition of front-wheel brakes: while the little Singer Ten of a few years earlier had cost £185, an Aston Martin rolling chassis was listed at £500 and a complete car at £650. But although the stage was set for Aston Martin to go into production, Martin was still concentrating on racing.

A completely new 16-valve, overhead-cam engine was designed, but it failed to produce any more power than the old side-valve. A twin-overhead-cam 16-valve engine, built in 1922 with support from the famous racing driver Count Louis Zborowski and fitted into two impressive Grand Prix 'voiturettes', was better, but still the side-valve often proved to have a better combination of pace and reliability. The side-valve's ultimate achievement came on 24 May, 1922, when a short-chassis Aston Martin called 'Bunny' ran head-to-head with a 1½-litre A.C. in a long-distance record-breaking run at Brooklands. A.C., going for the 12-hour record, assumed that Aston Martin were there to do the same and were amazed when Bunny continued running after 12 hours had passed. Instead the Aston Martin team was aiming for records in a '12 to 19 hours' class, which they duly achieved. In all, they set 25 'light-car' records and more importantly ten outright world speed records – an amazing feat.

Above The second of the 1922 French GP cars, with Clive Gallop at the wheel. Both cars retired from the race with magneto failure.

Below 'Green Pea' being driven by owner Neil Murray at a Brooklands Reunion. It is the oldest 'active' Aston Martin in the world.

Right '*Bunny*' *broke numerous speed records at Brooklands in 1923.*

Below The single-seater team car 'Razor Blade' seen outside the Brooklands Club House.

Above The twin-cam, 16-valve engine showing its troublesome vertical magneto (on the right).

Right This twin-cam, 16-valve single-seater was built for the 1925 JCC 200-mile race.

But Lionel Martin's focus on racing rather than production was taking its toll. Just a few dozen cars had been sold, and that wasn't paying for the racing activities. In 1924 control of the company passed to the Charnwood family, and the Hon. John Benson, later Lord Charnwood, designed an 8-valve, twin-cam engine to replace the 16-valve unit. Aston Martins appeared at the Motor Show at Olympia in 1925, but the company's financial position was dire. Production ceased and the receivers were called in. It would be almost a year before the Aston Martin name would reappear, on completely new cars built by a completely new company, Aston Martin Motors Limited.

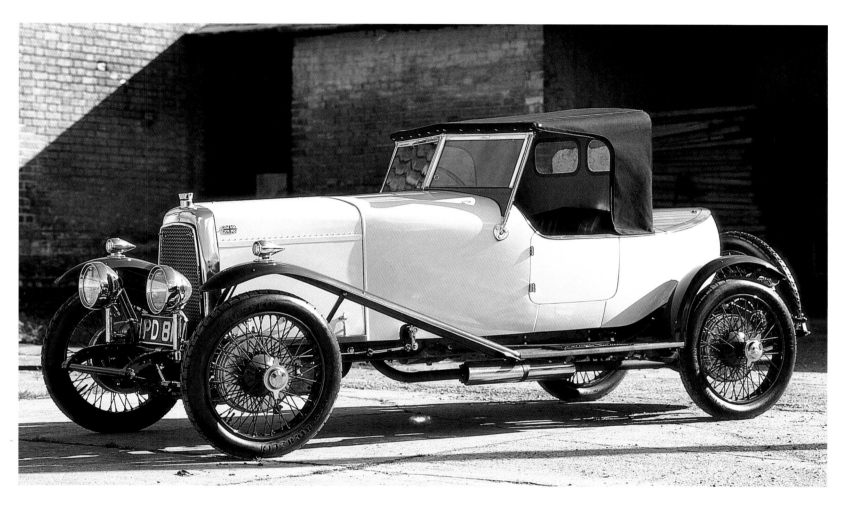

New power unit

The Charnwoods were joined in the new company by W.S. Renwick and A.C. 'Bert' Bertelli. Bertelli, an Italian-born engineer, had been General Manager of Enfield-Allday Motors until its parent company failed in 1922. After a spell working for Woolf Barnato, Bertelli had teamed up with Renwick, with a view to building engines and their own car, the R&B. Claude Hill was employed to design a single-overhead-cam 1½-litre 4-cylinder engine, which in 1926 was installed in an old Enfield-Allday chassis for testing. This new engine would be an ideal power unit for a new generation of Aston Martins.

New premises were found at Feltham in Middlesex, to the west of London. There the new Aston Martins slowly took shape, using the Claude Hill engine, a new chassis drawn up by Bertelli, and bodywork by Bertelli's brother Enrico, who had set up shop next door. At the 1927 Motor Show the new cars were announced: a long-chassis touring model (the T-Type, priced at £575) and a lower, shorter sporting version (the £495 S-Type), sharing Hill's 56bhp, 1494cc engine and good for 80mph (129km/h). Alongside them was a mock-up three-seater sports model that announced Aston Martin's intention to return to racing.

Bertelli was convinced that motor racing was an effective way of improving his cars, and to that end he had raced 10hp Enfield-Allday cars at Brooklands in the early 1920s – sometimes competing against Aston Martin. For 1928 two Aston 'team cars' were built to compete in the 24-hour race at Le Mans, and accordingly designated LM1 and LM2. For these Bertelli drew up a new chassis, six inches (152mm) shorter than the S-Type,

Above Lionel Martin concentrated on racing. Road cars, like this 1924 tourer, were rare.

1924 Sports 'Lionel Martin Series'	
Engine:	In-line 4-cylinder, side-valve
Bore/stroke:	66.5mm x 107mm
Capacity:	1486cc
Power:	45bhp @ 4000rpm
Fuel system:	Single carburettor
Gearbox:	4-speed manual
Chassis:	Steel channel
Body:	Aluminium alloy
Suspension:	Beam axles, semi-elliptic leaf springs
Brakes:	4-wheel drum brakes, mechanically operated
Top speed:	72mph (116km/h)
Acceleration:	0-50mph (80km/h) in 25sec

Above A.C. Bertelli in the 1930s. 'Bert' was responsible for the greatest pre-war Astons.

Right The Claude Hill-designed 1¹/₂ litre OHC engine seen here in the R&B 'Buzz-Box'.

Above Claude Hill, 1978.

Right 'T-Type' tourer of 1928.

underslung at the rear and fitted with lightweight aluminium-sleeved axles. The engine was tuned to raise power to 63bhp at 4750rpm, and fitted with a dry-sump lubrication system – a common feature on aeroplane engines, but a rarity in motoring circles at the time. Removing the oil-filled sump reduced the height of the engine, the oil being pumped in and out from a tank mounted prominently in front of the radiator under a louvred panel, where it could be easily cooled.

Though the new team cars looked purposeful, thanks to their low build and clean lines, Le Mans 1928 was not a success. Both cars broke axles while driving to the circuit – most teams drove their racing cars to the events in those days – and Bertelli, driving LM1, broke another axle in the race after hitting a concealed gulley. LM2 lasted 18 hours before breaking its gearlever. Aston Martin didn't return home entirely downcast, however, winning the Rudge-Whitworth prize for being the fastest 1½-litre cars over the first 20 laps of the race.

The dry-sump engine was offered in a production sports model, the International, announced at the 1928 Motor Show and in 1930 a high-compression 'Ulster' version was offered for £50 more. Racing continued, but sales were slow thanks to the Depression of the early 1930s, and Aston Martin still wasn't making money. First the Charnwoods and then Renwick left the company, Bertelli keeping Aston Martin afloat with help from friends and dealers. H.J. Aldington of Frazer Nash stepped in to finance the 1931 racing season, in return for which his company A.F.N. Ltd. took control of Aston Martin sales. Three new team cars were built, with higher compression cylinder heads (the 1½-litre engine was now developing 70bhp) and reinforced axles. The cars were fast in their class – they were timed at 90mph (145km/h) along the straight from Newtownards to Comber during the Ulster Tourist Trophy – but the season was a mixed one, and behind the scenes Bertelli was still struggling to ensure Aston Martin's survival as an independent company.

By the end of 1931 he had secured new money from Lance Prideaux-Brune of Winter Garden Garages, a London dealer. The International was modified to reduce costs; the Aston Martin-built gearbox was replaced by a Laycock unit, the worm-drive rear axle was replaced by an ENV spiral-bevel, and the chassis itself was redesigned to be easier and cheaper to make. As a result a 'New International' model went on sale early in 1932 at £475, fully £120 cheaper than the previous car, but it wasn't purely a cost-cutting exercise.

Above LM1, the first works racing car of the Bertelli era. It was later owned by S.C.H. Davis, who designed the Aston Martin badge – the black version of the badge, which he preferred, is still on the car today.

Below left 1931 International 2/4-seater with Perrot brakes.

1929 International

Engine:	In-line 4-cylinder, single-overhead-cam, dry sump
Bore/stroke:	69.3mm x 99mm
Capacity:	1494cc
Power:	56bhp @ 4250rpm
Fuel system:	Twin SU carburettors
Gearbox:	4-speed manual
Chassis:	Steel channel
Body:	Aluminium alloy
Suspension:	Beam axles, semi-elliptic leaf springs
Brakes:	4-wheel drum brakes, mechanically operated
Top speed:	78mph (126km/h)
Acceleration:	0-50mph (80km/h) in 20sec

Above Bertelli's engine reached its ultimate 1½-litre form in the 1935 team cars.

Below By 1934, when this Ulster was built, cable-operated front brakes had been adopted.

The New International was upgraded with cable-operated front brakes in place of the previous Perrot shaft system, and the overhead-cam engine now produced 60bhp at 4500rpm. Just 12 New Internationals were produced before the model was superseded, but the last of them saw another significant change: the introduction of a new Aston Martin badge, essentially the same as the one still in use today.

In 1931 Aston Martin had returned to Le Mans for the first time since 1928. Although two cars retired, Bertelli and Harvey battled on to finish fifth overall and first in class, in the process qualifying for the ninth Le Mans Biennial Cup, to be completed the following year. When they returned in 1932 with three new team cars based on the 'New International' chassis, Newsome and Widengren equalled Bertelli's achievement of the previous year, finishing fifth overall and first in class, with Bertelli and Pat Driscoll second in class and seventh overall. This result won them the Biennial Cup, awarded to the car with the best aggregate result over two years. To celebrate, a 'Le Mans' production model was introduced, with a much lower radiator and still higher compression ratio of 7.5:1, giving it 70bhp at 4750rpm and a top speed of 85mph (137km/h). Road testing the car in July, 1933, *The Autocar* remarked that the Le Mans was just about the nearest thing to a racing car that it was possible to buy 'for practical and general use on the road'. Sir Malcolm Campbell, however, is said to have described his Le Mans as 'slow' – but then he was the holder of the World Land Speed Record, at 272.465mph (438.490km/h)…

Full capacity

The Le Mans success attracted the attention of Sir Arthur Sutherland, a Newcastle shipping magnate, who injected much-needed capital into the company and installed his son Gordon alongside Bertelli as Joint Managing Director to look after sales. Such was the success of the Le Mans that the factory was now working to capacity, to the extent that there wasn't sufficient manpower available to produce new team cars for Le Mans, the previous year's cars having already been sold on to customers. Bertelli instead bought back one of the 1932 cars, borrowed another, and entered 'Mort' Morris-Goodall in his 1931 car to complete the team. That car retired, but the two 1932 cars (LM9 and LM10) finished a creditable fifth and seventh respectively, though they couldn't repeat the Biennial Cup success of the previous year.

Detail improvements to the cars were revealed for 1934, the obvious visual changes including a flat-topped scuttle and thermostatically-controlled radiator shutters, replacing the simple wire-mesh grille of earlier models. Under the skin a stiffer chassis and relocated Hartford friction dampers improved refinement. By the time of the Olympia Motor Show, the engine had been revised with a stiffer, fully counterbalanced crankshaft and improved cylinder head, raising power output to 73bhp at 4750rpm. Behind the scenes, engine development carried on, Aston's demonstrator being fitted with a 1.7-litre engine later in 1934, and then a full 2.0-litre unit the following year as the search for more power continued in earnest.

Three new team cars were built for 1934 using Mark II chassis, drilled to save weight and designated LM11, LM12 and LM14. Bertelli was superstitious, so there was no LM13. Even so, ill luck dogged Aston Martin at Le Mans that year, all three cars retiring with mechanical troubles. Though the cars' lightened chassis were legal at Le Mans, the regulations did not allow them at the Tourist Trophy, and all three were rebuilt for the Ards TT using standard undrilled chassis. At the same time Bertelli decided something had to be done to change Aston Martin's luck, so he ordered all three cars to be painted Italian racing red rather than the traditional green. It certainly seemed to work, as the three cars finished third, sixth and seventh and brought home the Team Prize.

To capitalize on this success an 'Ulster' production model was introduced: said to be ready to race, it came fitted with a narrow body (with fold-flat windscreen and distinctive horizontal spare wheel in the tail), tuned to give 80bhp and guaranteed to exceed 100mph (161km/h). Though just 21 were sold out of 166 Mark II cars (at £750 it was £140 more than the 'standard' Mark II 2/4-seater), the Ulster was one of the finest pre-war production Aston Martins.

Bertelli himself believed that the 1935 team cars were his best effort. These featured still more power, their 85bhp being the result of a higher compression ratio (achieved by using domed pistons), special fully-balanced Laystall crank, 1½in SU carburettors and a special camshaft. Again the three cars were painted Italian racing red. At Le Mans Charles Martin and Charles Brackenbury finished third overall (just 60 miles, 97km, behind the winning 4½-litre Lagonda of Hindmarsh and Fontes), won the 1½-litre class and brought home a second Biennial Cup. After a successful Le Mans and the previous year's showing at the TT, Aston Martin were optimistic for another good performance at Newtownards. Although new flexible oil pipes proved unreliable and prevented a strong finish for the red

1933 Le Mans	
Engine:	In-line 4-cylinder, single-overhead-cam, dry sump
Bore/stroke:	69.3mm x 99mm
Capacity:	1494cc
Power:	70bhp @ 4750rpm
Fuel system:	Twin SU carburettors
Gearbox:	4-speed manual
Chassis:	Steel channel
Body:	Aluminium alloy
Suspension:	Beam axles, semi-elliptic leaf springs
Brakes:	4-wheel drum brakes, cable front, mechanically operated rear
Top speed:	85mph (137km/h)
Acceleration:	0-50mph (80km/h) in 16sec

Below LM21 team car at a Nürburgring retro race. Pink Floyd drummer Nick Mason, the car's owner, is at the wheel.

Lagonda's Early Years

agonda was founded by expatriate American Wilbur Adams Gunn, born in Troy, Ohio in 1859. Gunn came to Britain towards the end of the 19th century – apparently to start a British offshoot of his brother-in-law's company, the Lagonda Manufacturing Co, which made steam equipment. Working out of the greenhouse at his home in Staines in Middlesex, he started building motorcycles which he called Lagondas, the name derived from the Shawnee Indian name for Buck Creek, which runs through Springfield, Ohio, where Gunn was raised. Lagonda branched out into three-wheelers in 1904, and by 1909 Gunn was building four-wheeled cars using Coventry-Simplex engines (as Aston Martin would a few years later) fitted to innovative chassis-less bodies. A larger, 16/18hp model followed, and this won the 1910 Moscow-St. Petersburg Reliability Trial. As a result it gained considerable Russian patronage, even from Tsar Nicholas II.

A new small car, the 11.1hp, was added to the range in 1913, and this car reappeared in slightly modified form after the war. Longer and heavier 11.9hp and 12/24 derivatives continued in production until 1925. But Gunn had died in 1920 and without his pioneering influence, Lagonda cars became more conservative.

By 1934 the tiny company was producing six distinct models, from the 1104cc Rapier up to the 4½-litre M45 and Rapide, and the strain was too much. Though a Rapide prepared by Lagonda dealers Fox and Nicholl won Le Mans outright in 1935, the financial situation did not improve, and Lagonda was forced to call in the receiver. It was saved by a London solicitor called Alan Good.

Good brought in W.O. Bentley – whose own company had been taken over by Rolls-Royce in 1930 – as Chief Designer. Bentley quickly produced the LG45, a revised M45, then set about designing a new car. This magnificent 4½-litre V12, launched at the 1937 Motor Show, was capable of over 100mph (161km/h) and 185 were built before production ended early in the Second World War. Bentley's thoughts then turned to a smaller Lagonda, which would see the light of day when hostilities ended.

Above This 1922 11.9hp Lagonda is typical of the company's early output.

Left and below Lagonda won Le Mans outright in 1935 with this M45R.

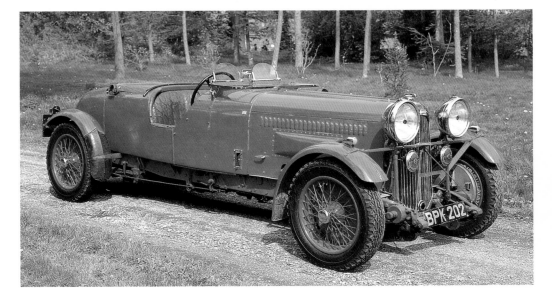

1934 Mark II

Engine:	In-line 4-cylinder, single-overhead-cam, dry sump
Bore/stroke:	69.3mm x 99mm
Capacity:	1494cc
Power:	73bhp @ 4750rpm
Fuel system:	Twin SU carburettors
Gearbox:	4-speed manual
Chassis:	Steel channel
Body:	Aluminium alloy
Suspension:	Beam axles, semi-elliptic leaf springs
Brakes:	4-wheel drum brakes, cable front, mechanically operated rear
Top speed:	84mph (135km/h)
Acceleration:	0-50mph (80km/h) in 15sec

Left 1934 Mark II with low-slung saloon body.

Below LM18, one of the successful 1935 cars.

1935 Ulster

Engine:	In-line 4-cylinder, single-overhead-cam, dry sump
Bore/stroke:	69.3mm x 99mm
Capacity:	1494cc
Power:	85bhp @ 5250rpm
Fuel system:	Twin SU carburettors
Gearbox:	4-speed manual
Chassis:	Steel channel
Body:	Aluminium alloy body
Suspension:	Beam axles, semi-elliptic leaf springs
Brakes:	4-wheel drum brakes, cable front, mechanically operated rear
Top speed:	100mph (161km/h)
Acceleration:	0-50mph (80km/h) in 12sec

Above Cockpit of the very original 1934 Ulster owned by the Aston Martin Owners Club.

Right and below St John Horsfall's 2-litre Speed Model, 'the black car', in which he won the 1946 Belgian GP.

cars, Aston Martin still finished fourth, fifth and 11th to hold on to the Team Prize for a second year.

Rumours of a bigger engines – which the factory had been testing since 1934 – were confirmed when a pair of 2.0-litre cars were entered for Le Mans in 1936, alongside a team of three 1½-litre cars. Sadly Le Mans that year was cancelled at the last minute due to a national strike and political turmoil in France, and the 2.0-litre team cars were sold on to private competitors, depriving Bertelli of his last chance of Le Mans glory. While he was keen to keep on racing, the Sutherlands were more inclined to spend Aston Martin's money developing road cars, and so Bertelli resigned that year, having put Aston Martin firmly on the motoring map. His erstwhile assistant Claude Hill took over as the company's Chief Designer.

Beyond Bertelli

By August 2.0-litre cars were in production, the 'Speed Model' being a replica of the cars built for Le Mans, on a similar chassis to the Ulster but with Lockheed hydraulic brakes, extra cable location being fitted to the front axle to prevent the springs 'winding up' under heavy braking. A 'bread and butter' 15/98 was also offered using a detuned, wet-sump version of the same 2.0-litre engine which, compared to the 1½-litre, was expanded both in bore and stroke at 78 x 102mm – a figure which makes more sense when expressed as 3 x 4in. While the Le Mans cars developed over 100bhp, the 15/98 got its designation from its RAC horsepower rating (15hp) and its true power output of 98bhp at 5000rpm. When Bertelli left and the connection between Aston Martin and E. Bertelli was severed, Abbotts and Abbey both built bodies. Until then most models had been fitted with cycle wings mounted on the brake back-plates, which meant that they went up and down with the

1938 15/98 drophead coupé	
Engine:	In-line 4-cylinder, single-overhead-cam
Bore/stroke:	78mm x 102mm
Capacity:	1950cc
Power:	98bhp @ 5000rpm
Fuel system:	Twin SU carburettors
Gearbox:	4-speed manual
Chassis:	Steel channel
Body:	Aluminium alloy
Suspension:	Beam axles, semi-elliptic leaf springs
Brakes:	4-wheel drum brakes, hydraulically operated
Top speed:	85mph (137km/h)
Acceleration:	0-50mph (80km/h) in 14sec

Above left 1937 15/98 2-litre four-door saloon.

Left Radical 'Type C' body was unpopular.

Above This 1938 15/98 short-chassis 2/4-seater was Aston Martin's demonstrator.

suspension and the front wings turned as the wheels were steered. But the 15/98 was different, as flowing, chassis-mounted wings were fitted to the standard bodies.

Though the 15/98 proved popular, the Speed Model was a slow seller, and by 1938 the factory still had unsold chassis that had been built in 1936. In an effort to clear them, a radical new 'aerodynamic' body was evolved, with flowing wings and (on most of the cars) close-set headlights fitted behind the wire-mesh radiator grille. But the new 'Type C' proved little quicker than the Speed Model, and sales remained slow as war loomed. Sutherland had realized that a new model would be needed, and Claude Hill was already working on it.

DB Takes Control

Above The construction method used for the body of the 15/98 saloon 'Donald Duck' would reappear on the wartime Atom.

Previous page 1953 Aston Martin DB2/4.

Below The Atom prototype's shape had much in common with the pre-war Type C.

Opposite Under the skin the Atom was completely different to previous Astons, and would form the basis for post-war models.

Gordon Sutherland and Claude Hill planned to replace the 15/98 and Speed Model with a radically different car, and in 1939 they built the prototype: a car called the Atom.

Previous Aston Martins had been based on a traditional ladder-type chassis – two channel-section members running the length of the car, braced at intervals – with a separate and essentially unstressed body mounted on the top. The Atom was constructed very differently, more along aircraft lines. The chassis was made from square and rectangular section tubes, and welded to this was a lighter tubular framework for the body, the body tubes contributing some stiffness to the chassis and thus allowing the main chassis members to be lighter without compromising the stiffness of the whole car. Square and rectangular section tubes were used because they were easier to weld neatly together than round tubes.

Aluminium alloy body panels were fitted to the framework, the styling of the car continuing the 'aerodynamic' theme which had begun in 1938. A 15/98 had been rebuilt by the factory with a fastback saloon body (a car soon nicknamed 'Donald Duck') using a similar method of body construction to the Atom, but without using the bodywork to stiffen the chassis. The unloved Type C followed, and the Atom's shape had much in common with that. Neither car had traditional separate wings or freestanding headlights; the Type C hid its headlights behind an oval wire-mesh grille, while the Atom mounted them flush with the bodywork, the grille consisting only of a dozen slots in the front panel either side of a chrome trim strip. Sutherland favoured closed cars, so the Atom was a

close-coupled four-door sporting saloon, the front and rear doors on either side being hung from the central pillar. The use of flat glass dictated that the windscreen was split vertically in the centre, the windscreen wipers being mounted in the roof panel above the screen.

The running gear, too, departed from traditional practice. While a conventional beam axle suspended on semi-elliptic leaf springs was used at the rear, the axle itself incorporated the new Salisbury hypoid bevel final drive, which allowed the prop-shaft line to be lower. For the first time on an Aston Martin, the front suspension was independent, with a cast trailing arm on each side suspended by a coil spring. Hydraulic lever arm dampers were used, arranged so that their arms moved parallel to the suspension arms. The steering incorporated a divided track-rod to reduce bump-steer.

Wartime interruption

A Cotal electric gearbox was fitted, a four-speed epicyclic geartrain controlled by solenoids which were themselves controlled using a tiny dash-mounted gearlever. Initially the Atom was powered by a 15/98 engine while Claude Hill worked on a new 2.0-litre pushrod unit. However, the war intervened, Aston Martin went to work for the Ministry of Aircraft production, and engine development slowed to a crawl. Meanwhile Gordon Sutherland used the Atom extensively during the war, the car proving to have good performance and an excellent ride.

1944 Atom prototype	
Engine:	In-line 4-cylinder, pushrod overhead-valve
Bore/stroke:	82.55mm x 92mm
Capacity:	1970cc
Power:	90bhp @ 4750rpm
Fuel system:	Twin SU carburettors
Gearbox:	4-speed Cotal electric
Chassis:	Tubular steel frame
Body:	Aluminium alloy body
Suspension:	Front: trailing arms with coil springs. Rear: live axle, semi-elliptic leaf springs
Brakes:	4-wheel drum brakes, hydraulically operated
Top speed:	105mph (169km/h)
Acceleration:	0-50mph (80km/h) in 18sec

Above Gordon Sutherland, who led Aston Martin from the mid-1930s to the David Brown takeover in 1947.

Hill's engine was ready by 1944. Again it was an in-line, 4-cylinder unit, but instead of the pre-war engine's overhead-cam layout the new engine had its valves operated by pushrods and rockers, the camshaft mounted low and driven by a chain from the five-bearing crankshaft. The valve arrangement itself was unusual, with the inlet valves placed vertically above the cylinders and the exhaust valves angled to one side in an effort to improve exhaust efficiency and thus produce more power. With a bigger bore and shorter stroke than the pre-war 2.0-litre, the new engine was smoother and more free-revving, and despite a lower compression ratio than the pre-war 15/98 (in deference to poor-quality wartime 'pool' petrol), it still produced 90bhp and gave the Atom a top speed in excess of 100mph (161km/h).

It was not, though, a production car. Much work needed to be done before the Atom would be a commercial proposition and more capital was needed. Gordon Sutherland needed a new investor and in 1946 he placed an advertisement in the *Times* newspaper, offering the company for sale.

The advert was seen by industrialist David Brown, who visited Feltham and drove the Atom, which by then was powered by Claude Hill's new pushrod engine. Brown was impressed by the car's roadholding but considered it under-powered. In later years he explained that when he bought Aston Martin in February 1947, it was as a hobby, rather than a commercial enterprise. The company cost him £20,000.

Sutherland and Hill both stayed on as directors, and as Britain shivered in the coldest winter anyone could remember, they set about the task of creating a production car out of the promising Atom prototype. 'D.B.' wanted the new car to be a drophead, so Claude

Right The neat interior of the Atom prototype.

Hill redesigned the chassis, using twin side tubes to make up for some of the stiffness lost by removing the fixed roof. An anti-roll bar was added to the front suspension, and at the rear the leaf springs were replaced by coils, axle location being by trailing arms and a Panhard rod. A conventional David Brown gearbox was fitted in place of the Atom's Cotal electric unit.

D.B. buys Lagonda

While development of the new Aston Martin got under way, David Brown was approached by Tony Scratchard, who ran the Lagonda distributor in Bradford. Scratchard urged Brown to buy Lagonda. Brown wasn't interested, but when Lagonda went into liquidation D.B. discovered that he knew the liquidator through previous business dealings, so he agreed to look again. He met W.O. Bentley at Staines and examined the twin-cam, 6-cylinder engine that W.O. was developing for a new small Lagonda. D.B. immediately saw that the twin-cam engine was a tried and tested design that could power Aston Martins, but three large bids for Lagonda had already been received – from Armstrong-Siddeley, Jaguar and the Rootes Group. As Brown later recalled, he thought they were for far more than the company was worth, and he put in a much lower offer.

All three of the larger bids were withdrawn later in the year as industry struggled to come to terms with fuel shortages and Chancellor Hugh Dalton's 'emergency budget'. The Staines factory buildings were sold to the diesel engine manufacturer Petters, and D.B. was able to pick up the rest of Lagonda for just £52,500. He leased some hangars at Hanworth airfield at Feltham, just up the road from Aston Martin, and installed everything there.

Cross-fertilization between Aston Martin and Lagonda began almost immediately. Frank Feeley, Lagonda's stylist, began work on a body for the new Aston Martin blending extravagant curves with an updated version of the pre-war Aston Martin grille. Meanwhile, test driver St John 'Jock' Horsfall persuaded Brown to enter a racing version of their new chassis in the Spa 24-hour race. Brown remained unconvinced, but allowed a

Above Lagonda and Aston Martin stylist *Frank Feeley.*

Below The 'Spa Special' won the 24-hour race at Spa in 1948 – to David Brown's surprise.

car to be built with a simple racing body, and to his surprise Horsfall and Leslie Johnson won the event outright. At the Motor Show of 1948 – the first London show since the war had ended – the new Aston Martin Two-Litre Sports was revealed to the public, and sitting alongside it was a 'Spa Replica', actually the Spa-winning car rebuilt with a new body.

No Spa Replicas were sold, and there were only 14 production versions of what in retrospect was known as the DB1. The car certainly had presence, but Feeley's styling wasn't universally praised, and as always the car was expensive – particularly when compared to the astonishing new Jaguar XK120, also launched at the 1948 show. But producing any cars at all was an achievement in the late 1940s, with 'pool' petrol, shortages, rationing and power-cuts to cope with. Like many other manufacturers of the time Aston Martin found themselves unable to buy steel until they had exported cars, and without steel they couldn't build cars to export. The problem was solved by David Brown, who diverted steel from other areas of the group to get Aston Martin going.

To get Lagonda going, too. W.O. Bentley's '2½-litre' Lagonda, actually powered by a 2.6-litre version of the LB6 twin-cam that David Brown had admired, had been announced as far back as September 1945. Willie Watson had drawn up the engine plan under Bentley's supervision, using the now-classic layout of six in-line cylinders, twin chain-

Below The 2-litre Sports, in retrospect known as the DB1, was the first David Brown Aston.

Opposite top Jaguar's XK120 was much cheaper than the Aston Martin, and its styling was generally regarded as superior.

Opposite W.O. Bentley's Lagonda was modified before production began in 1949.

1948 Two-Litre Sports 'DB1'

Engine:	In-line 4-cylinder, pushrod overhead-valve
Bore/stroke:	82.55mm x 92mm
Capacity:	1970cc
Power:	90bhp @ 4750rpm
Fuel system:	Twin SU carburettors
Gearbox:	4-speed David Brown manual
Chassis:	Tubular steel frame
Body:	Aluminium alloy
Suspension:	Front: trailing arms with coil springs and anti-rollbar. Rear: coil-sprung live axle located by trailing arms and Panhard rod
Brakes:	4-wheel drum brakes, hydraulically operated
Top speed:	93mph (150km/h)
Acceleration:	0-60mph (97km/h) in 14sec

driven overhead camshafts and hemispherical combustion chambers with valves at 30 degrees to the vertical. The crankcase extended well below the centreline of the main bearings; to get the crankshaft in, each of the bearings (except that at the front) was carried in a pair of semi-circular, duralumin carriers – nicknamed 'cheeses' – which mated with large circular holes in the block.

Three prototype Lagondas had been built, but the ailing company had been unable to raise the capital or find the materials to put it into production. Under the D.B. banner things were different. After some modification – the cruciform chassis was reinforced, and the Cotal gearbox specified by Bentley was dropped in favour of a David Brown manual box – production of the car began in early 1949.

Lagonda power

Below The fifth DB2 built, originally fitted with a 2-litre engine but later the development car for the 2.6-litre Lagonda LB6 unit.

Opposite The first drophead coupé DB2, originally owned by David Brown.

D.B., of course, intended the LB6 engine to power the next Aston Martin. Three new DB2 coupés were built for Le Mans, with chassis based on the DB1 but nine inches (229mm) shorter in wheelbase. Frank Feeley penned a clean two-door, fastback shape which solved the problem of engine access with a full-width fold-forward front end. Two cars were powered by the 2.0-litre DB1 engine and one was fitted with the LB6. Claude Hill, who had been working on a six-cylinder version of his pushrod engine, was understandably

annoyed that the Lagonda engine was being fitted instead; Brown was keen to use the running, tested Lagonda engine rather than Hill's as-yet-untried unit. As a result Hill left Aston Martin, and his friend Jock Horsfall soon followed.

At Le Mans the LB6 hardly covered itself in glory. A defective water pump caused it to lose its water after just six laps, and the car had to be retired. Worse was to come for Aston Martin: on Sunday morning Pierre Marechal crashed one of the 2.0-litre cars at White House and was badly injured. The other 2.0-litre soldiered on to finish seventh, but Marechal died the following day. It was to be the only fatal accident ever suffered by the Aston Martin's works team.

The Spa 24-hours, the following month, was a very different and much happier story. Leslie Johnson and Charles Brackenbury were back in the 2.6-litre car they had shared at Le Mans, and they brought it home third overall. Horsfall drove the entire 24 hours single-handed (with Paul Frère on stand-by just in case he couldn't go the distance) to finish fourth in his privately-entered pre-war Speed Model, with the Nick Haines/Lance Macklin 2.0-litre DB2 fifth.

Work began on a production model shortly afterwards. The DB2's roof and bonnet lines were raised to produce a more practical motor car, which was displayed at the New York Motor Show in April 1950 having been announced to the press a few days earlier. David Brown also sanctioned a proper racing programme for 1950 (the story of which is told in the next chapter) and racing development of the LB6 engine enabled Aston Martin to offer a higher-output engine option under the 'Vantage' name by the end of the year. By 1951 a drophead coupé version had been announced and the DB2's styling had also been

1950 DB2	
Engine:	In-line 6-cylinder, twin-overhead-cam
Bore/stroke:	78mm x 90mm
Capacity:	2580cc
Power:	105bhp @ 5000rpm
Fuel system:	Twin SU carburettors
Gearbox:	4-speed David Brown manual
Chassis:	Tubular steel frame
Body:	Aluminium alloy
Suspension:	Front: trailing arms with coil springs and anti-roll bar. Rear: coil-sprung live axle located by twin trailing arms and Panhard rod
Brakes:	4-wheel drum brakes, hydraulically operated
Top speed:	110mph (177km/h)
Acceleration:	0-60mph (97km/h) in 12.4sec

David Brown the Man, David Brown the Group

The David Brown who bought Aston Martin in February 1947 was the grandson of the founder of the David Brown group of companies. Started as a pattern-making business in 1860, the company developed into gear manufacture, becoming a major supplier to industry by the time of the founder's death in 1903. David Brown had three sons, all of whom were involved with the family business: Percy Brown became Chairman until his death in 1931, when he was succeeded by his brother Frank.

Frank's son David started at the bottom as an engineering apprentice at David Brown Gears in Huddersfield. Even then he was interested in speed machinery. Apprentices clocked on a 7.30am, and to ensure he wasn't late his father bought him a motorcycle. Brown tried to get a Harley-Davidson, but had to settle for a 1000cc V-twin Reading Standard, another big American machine. Brown tuned it, increasing the compression ratio, lightening the flywheel and fitting narrower

Above Sir David Brown.

mudguards. Brown and the bike competed in hillclimbs at Sutton Bank, Yorkshire and the Axe Edge, Derbyshire, recording fastest time of the day at Axe Edge. That led to an offer of a place in a motorcycle TT team as a reserve rider, but that idea was vetoed by Brown's father.

David Brown's first taste of management was at one of the group's subsidiaries, the loss-making Keighley

Gears, which Brown turned into a profitable company. He then reorganized a business in France, and returned in 1931 to become joint Managing Director of the group alongside W.S. Roe. Within weeks Roe was taken ill, and he died in August 1932, leaving David Brown in charge of the group at the tender age of 28.

Under Brown's control, Aston Martin was a useful promotional tool for the whole David Brown group. While Aston Martin benefited from financial security and access to materials and techniques it could not otherwise have obtained, the group basked in the reflected glory of Aston Martin's racing successes.

Sir David – he was knighted in 1968 for services to industry – sold Aston Martin in 1972, retiring to Monte Carlo. The family's interests in the David Brown group as a whole were ended by a management buyout in 1990. The group was floated on the London Stock Exchange in 1993, the same year that David Brown died. He was 89.

Right Ivor Silverstone's concours-winning 1951 DB2. Note the neat grille and lack of bonnet-side vents compared to the earlier cars.

Opposite Two small rear seats were squeezed into the DB2/4 of 1953.

tidied, with the three separate parts of the early DB1-style grille blended into a single shape which has been a feature of Aston Martins ever since.

The DB2 proved popular and 411 were built, more than double the number of any previous Aston Martin model, in the three years before it was replaced by the DB2/4. Removing the cross-bracing above the rear axle had allowed space for two rear seats to be fitted and a lift-up rear door – which today we would call a hatchback – was let into the rear bodywork for access to the luggage space. Further revisions to the body (now supplied by Mulliners of Birmingham) included separate bumpers – the DB2 had nothing more than chrome rubbing strips – and a single-piece windscreen. To counteract a small increase in weight the 125bhp Vantage-spec engine was standard when the DB2/4 was announced at the Motor Show in October 1953. A new Lagonda with bodywork by the Tickford coachbuilding company and a bigger 3.0-litre engine was introduced at the same time. This race-bred 140bhp power unit went into the DB2/4 the following summer, lessons learned from the competition cars again feeding back into production.

Detail changes produced the Mark II version of the DB2/4 in 1955. The roofline was raised slightly, a chrome strip was inserted above the windscreen and tiny fins sprouted from the rear wings in accordance with mid-1950s fashions. The engine bay side panels were also fixed to the body instead of the bonnet because the DB2's fold-forward front end had proved to be heavy and prone to shake on rough roads.

Body supply switched from Mulliners, which had been taken over by Standard-Triumph, to Tickford, which David Brown soon added to his empire. This caused some concern at Coventry-based Alvis, who had relied on Tickford and Mulliner for bodies and

1953 DB2/4	
Engine:	In-line 6-cylinder, twin-overhead-cam
Bore/stroke:	78mm x 90mm
Capacity:	2580cc
Power:	125bhp @ 5000rpm
Fuel system:	Twin SU carburettors
Gearbox:	4-speed David Brown manual
Chassis:	Tubular steel frame
Body:	Aluminium alloy
Suspension:	Front: trailing arms with coil springs and anti-roll bar. Rear: coil-sprung live axle located by twin trailing arms and Panhard rod
Brakes:	4-wheel drum brakes, hydraulically operated
Top speed:	114mph (183km/h)
Acceleration:	0-60mph (97km/h) in 12.6sec

Above The Lagondas of the 1950s were elegant, but slow-selling. This is a 1953 3.0-litre drophead.

Right Chrome strips highlight the revised bonnet and higher roof of the DB2/4 Mark II.

Left All DB2 models provided excellent access to the engine and front suspension. This is a DB2/4, with a Vantage-spec engine.

1955 DB2/4 Mark II

Engine:	In-line 6-cylinder, twin-overhead-cam
Bore/stroke:	83mm x 90mm
Capacity:	2922cc
Power:	140bhp @ 5000rpm
Fuel system:	Twin SU carburettors
Gearbox:	4-speed David Brown manual
Chassis:	Tubular steel frame
Body:	Aluminium alloy
Suspension:	Front: trailing arms with coil springs and anti-roll bar. Rear: coil-sprung live axle located by twin trailing arms and Panhard rod
Brakes:	4-wheel drum brakes, hydraulically operated
Top speed:	120mph (193km/h)
Acceleration:	0-60mph (97km/h) in 9.5sec

Left Simple elegance: the DB2/4 Mark II's understated interior.

Above The DB Mark III's instruments were grouped in front of the driver.

Below The DB Mark III featured a useful 'hatchback' rear door.

suddenly found both companies taken over. Production of Aston Martins and Lagondas now moved to Tickford's works at Newport Pagnell in Buckinghamshire, leaving Feltham to concentrate on service, development and racing.

Revised engine

Racing proved to be the inspiration for the restyled Mark III which was introduced at the Geneva show in March 1957 and produced for export only until the London Motor Show in October that year. Theoretically it was a DB2/4 Mark III, but almost everyone referred to it as the DB Mark III – except for Ian Fleming, who called it a 'DB III' as we will see later. In addition to a grille reminiscent of the DB3S racing car, the Mark III had a neater tail and some of the Mark II's unnecessary chromework had been deleted. A new fascia panel reflected the shape of the grille and grouped all the instruments in front of the driver for the first time.

Under the bonnet there was a major improvement: Polish engineer Tadek Marek had been hired from Austin to work on a new Aston Martin engine, but first he had redesigned the existing 3.0-litre. The block, crankshaft, inlet and exhaust manifolds, oil pump and timing chain were all new, and the new engine – designated the DBA – was said to produce 162bhp at 5500rpm. Higher-performance derivatives became available later, culminating in 1959 in a 'competition' spec called DBC, developing 214bhp and listed at an extra £350 on top of the Mark III's basic price of £3076. This included the UK Purchase Tax of the

Left British-registered DB Mark III drophead coupé, pictured on a European rally.

Left Tadek Marek redesigned the 3.0-litre engine for the DB Mark III. This is one of only ten cars with the 195bhp 'DBB' engine.

1957 DB Mark III	
Engine:	In-line 6-cylinder, twin-overhead-cam
Bore/stroke:	78mm x 90mm
Capacity:	2580cc
Power:	162bhp @ 5500rpm
Fuel system:	Twin SU carburettors
Gearbox:	4-speed David Brown manual
Chassis:	Tubular steel frame
Body:	Aluminium alloy
Suspension:	Front: trailing arms with coil springs and anti-roll bar. Rear: coil-sprung live axle located by twin trailing arms and Panhard rod
Brakes:	Disc front, drum rear, servo assisted
Top speed:	119mph (192km/h)
Acceleration:	0-60mph (97km/h) in 9.3sec

time which amounted to more than £1000. Drum brakes were still standard initially, but Girling discs were an option, and they were fitted as standard after the first 100 cars had been made. Other options included overdrive (from 1958) and Borg Warner automatic transmission (from 1959).

The Mark III continued in production until 1959, 550 being built – a longer production run than had been planned, as its DB4 replacement was slow to get going. And anyway, Aston Martin had its mind on something else: sporting success.

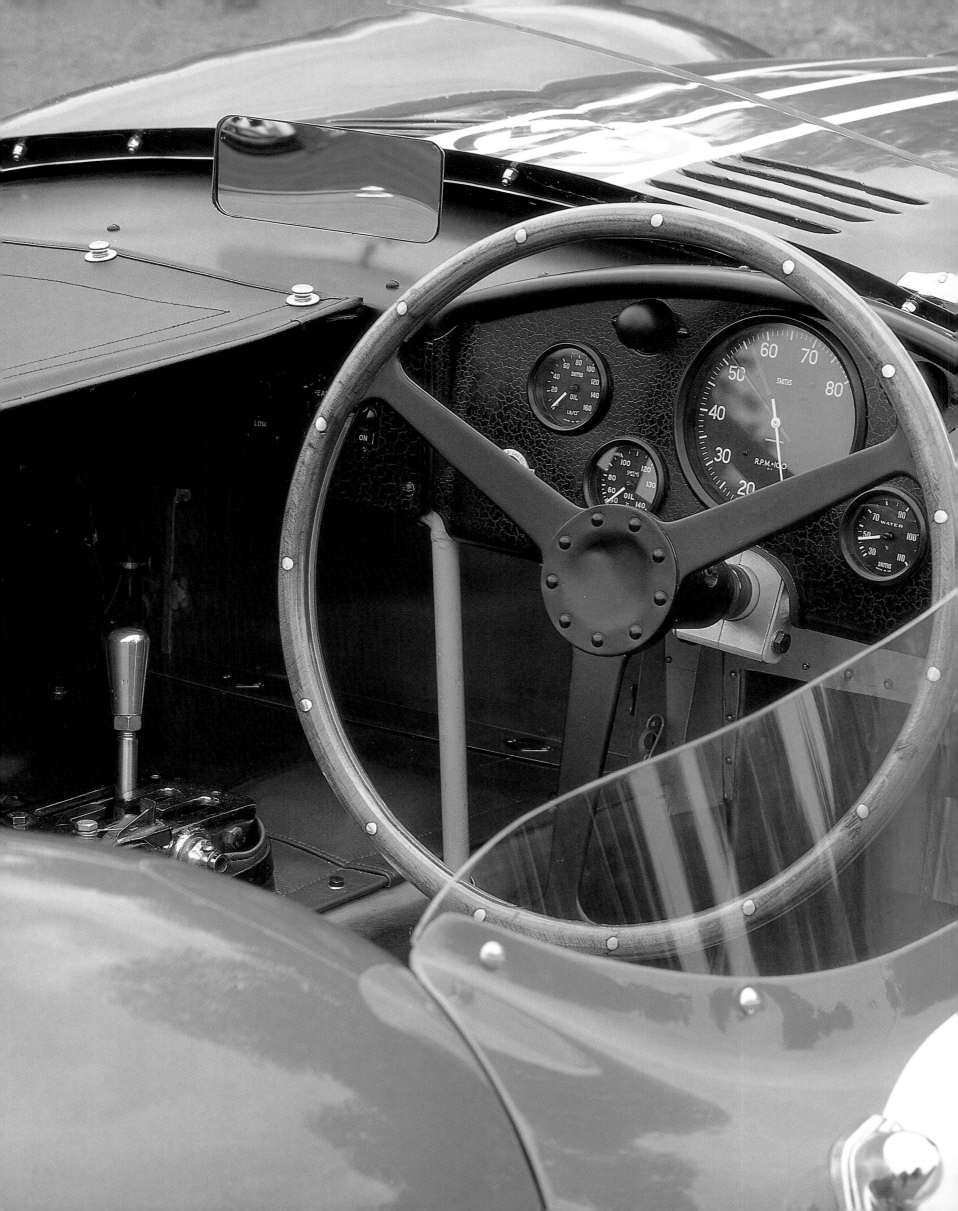

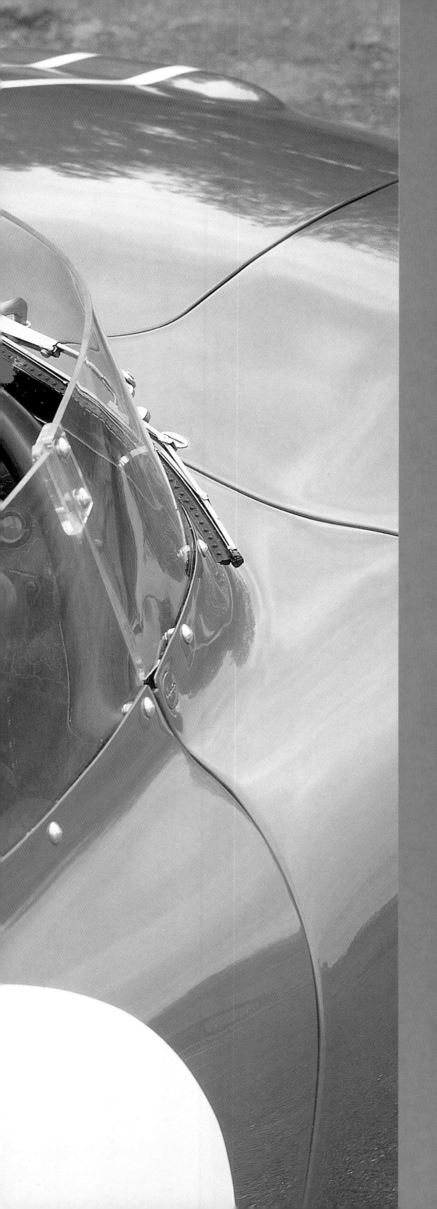

Improving
the Breed

While Jock Horsfall and Leslie Johnson had been busy winning the 1948 Spa 24-hour race for Aston Martin, David Brown had been keeping an eye on another car in the same race, an ex-Dick Seaman 2.0-litre Speed Model prepared by Monaco Motors in Watford. It pressed the factory Aston hard until a mistake after 20 hours put it off the road and out of contention. Running the team – 'pretty efficiently', Brown noted – was John Wyer.

When the prototype DB2's impressive performance at Spa the following year prompted David Brown to sanction a fuller racing programme for 1950, he sought out Wyer to run the team. Monaco Motors had been sold and Wyer was wondering what to do next. Brown told him he needed someone to run Aston's works team for one season, and that suited Wyer perfectly. He was to remain at Aston Martin for 13 years…

Three new DB2 team cars – registered VMF63, VMF64 and VMF65 – were built for the Le Mans 24-hour race, all three very much in standard specification apart from a slightly higher compression ratio, a freer-flowing exhaust and less interior trim. David Brown had already re-signed 1949 drivers Charles Brackenbury and Lance Macklin, and Wyer completed the team with George Abecassis, Jack Fairman, Reg Parnell and Eric Thompson. (D.B. himself toyed with the idea of driving, but wasn't experienced enough to be allowed an entry at Le Mans.) Disaster struck before the team even got to the circuit.

The three team cars were driven to Le Mans in company with 'Sweatbox', the 2.6-litre prototype that had finished third at Spa the previous year. At night and in heavy rain, Jack Fairman put VMF65 off the road near Rouen. His very pregnant wife, who was with him in the car, had to be taken to hospital. VMF65 was too badly bent to race, so the Sweatbox was run instead but broke its crankshaft after eight laps. The other two cars fared much better, Macklin and Abecassis bringing VMF64 home fifth and winning the 3.0-litre class, Brackenbury and Parnell in VMF63 finishing sixth overall and second in class. In addition, VMF64 won the 'Index of Performance'.

At the Silverstone sports car race in August, Parnell and Thompson were joined by the French ace Raymond Sommer, replacing the injured Macklin in VMF64, and Sommer

Previous page Cockpit of 1957 DBR2.

Right 'Sweatbox', the 1949 Le Mans DB2, at a Pebble Beach concours. It is far tidier now than when it was a working racing car.

Opposite The Reg Parnell/David Hampshire 'lightweight' DB2 built for Le Mans in 1951, where it finished seventh. Note the extra, roof-mounted wiper, and the red pit-signalling light on the rear pillar.

nearly won the 3.0-litre class. The season ended with another good race at the Dundrod Tourist Trophy where Parnell, Abecassis and Macklin occupied the top three positions in the 3.0-litre class.

For 1951 the plan was to create a proper racing machine, the DB3, using the DB2's engine. David Brown hired Professor Robert Eberan von Eberhorst, Chief Engineer with the pre-war Auto Union Grand Prix team, to design the car. Work started in December 1950, Eberan scheming a twin-tube chassis along similar lines to the Auto Union, though the Aston would retain its front-mounted engine. Wyer soon realized that the car would not be ready for Le Mans in 1951, and set about building two new DB2s as an alternative.

1951 DB2 Team Car	
Engine:	In-line 6-cylinder, twin-overhead-cam
Bore/stroke:	78mm x 90mm
Capacity:	2580cc
Power:	138bhp @ 5500rpm
Fuel system:	Triple Weber carburettors
Gearbox:	4-speed David Brown manual
Chassis:	Tubular steel frame
Body:	Aluminium alloy
Suspension:	Front: trailing arms with coil springs and anti-roll bar. Rear: coil-sprung live axle located by twin trailing arms and Panhard rod
Brakes:	Disc front, drum rear, servo assisted
Top speed:	132mph (212km/h)
Acceleration:	0-60mph (97km/h) in 10sec

These had drilled chassis members, plexiglass side windows and body panels made from 18-gauge aluminium alloy instead of 16-gauge, resulting in a weight saving of around 450lb (204kg). Alloy cylinder heads were tried on the two cars at Silverstone in May (Parnell winning the class, Abecassis retiring with gearbox trouble) but the DB2s reverted to iron heads for Le Mans, where triple Weber carburettors were fitted and the power output increased to 138bhp. Wyer had hoped at least one DB3 would be available for Le Mans, but it was nowhere near ready, so a third DB2 – VMF64, which David Brown had been using as a road car – was modified to somewhere between standard and 'lightweight' spec. Macklin and Thompson were disappointed to get 'last year's' car instead of a new lightweight, but ended up winning the class and finishing third overall behind the Walker/Whitehead Jaguar and Meyrat/Mairesse Talbot-Lago. Abecassis and Brian Shaw-Taylor were fifth, second in class and 'leading lightweight', while Parnell and David

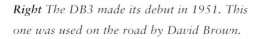

Above Lance Macklin and Eric Thompson were disappointed to be driving VMF64 instead of a new lightweight DB2 at Le Mans in 1951 – but brought it home in third place and won the class!

Right The DB3 made its debut in 1951. This one was used on the road by David Brown.

Hampshire finished seventh overall and third in class. And to give Aston Martin something really to celebrate, two privately entered DB2s had also competed and both finished – Mann/Morris-Goodall 10th and Clark/Scott 13th.

DB3 debut

At the Dundrod TT in September the DB3 finally made its debut, but retired when an oil leak from the new magnesium sump caused a bearing to fail. A full season followed in 1952, but good results were rare. A second/third/fourth finish at Silverstone in May set a good precedent, but the Monaco Grand Prix (which was for sports cars that year) saw two cars go out with engine trouble and another crash. At Le Mans just a couple of weeks later all three cars went out with axle failures. Then, at the Goodwood Nine Hours in August, the shunted Monaco car – which had been rebuilt in a hurry by Paris coachbuilder Henri Chapron, and which sported a 'Manx' tail as a result – was badly burned in a fire during refuelling. Despite the dramas in the pits, another DB3 driven by Pat Griffith and Peter Collins won the race.

Above The DB3 later used 2.9-litre engines.

Below DB3/3 was crashed at Monaco in 1952, then erupted in flames during refuelling in the Goodwood Nine Hours later that year.

1952 DB3

Engine:	In-line 6-cylinder, twin-overhead-cam
Bore/stroke:	83mm x 90mm
Capacity:	2922cc
Power:	163bhp @ 5500rpm
Fuel system:	Triple Weber carburettors
Gearbox:	4-speed David Brown manual
Chassis:	Steel twin-tube
Body:	Aluminium alloy
Suspension:	Front: trailing arms with transverse torsion bars and anti-roll bar. Rear: de Dion with transverse torsion bars and Panhard rod
Brakes:	4-wheel drum brakes, inboard at rear, hydraulically operated
Top speed:	140mph (225km/h)
Acceleration:	0-60mph (97km/h) in 9.0sec (estimated)

Though the DB3 was now running with a big-bore, 2.9-litre engine, it was really too big and heavy to be fully competitive – it had turned out to be only a fraction lighter than Wyer's 'lightweight' DB2s. In January 1953 Willie Watson suggested reshaping the chassis tubes so that the driver could be seated between them, instead of on top, and reducing the thicknesses of tubing. Frank Feeley designed a new body with cutaway front wheel arches, intended to provide an exit path for hot air from the engine bay, but in the process making the new DB3S a spectacularly pretty car. Weighing in 165lb (75kg) lighter than DB3, the new car was testing at Monza in May, just a few days after Parnell had brought a DB3 home fifth in the Mille Miglia – despite driving with broken suspension and by controlling the car on the ignition switch after the throttle cable broke…

Left Interior of the DB3S – note the huge rev-counter right in front of the driver.

Below Until 1955 the DB3S engine used a single-plug cylinder head.

DB3S disappoints

The DB3S made its debut at Le Mans, but it was an inauspicious start – all three cars retired. Parnell made an uncharacteristic unforced error, crashing the car at Tertre Rouge after just 16 laps. Abecassis, partnered by Roy Salvadori, retired with a slipping clutch, while the engine failed in the Poore/Thompson DB3S.

Keen to atone for his error, Parnell asked to borrow the prototype DB3S – now relegated to the role of spares car – to drive in the British Empire Trophy in the Isle of Man. David Brown agreed, so Parnell drove the car back from Le Mans, picked up mechanic Eric Hind from Feltham, and drove to Liverpool, where the car was put on a boat for the Isle of Man. John Wyer flew in for practice, where Reg set the fastest time. This was then beaten by Stirling Moss in a Jaguar C-Type and Reusch in a Ferrari. Parnell went out again, broke the lap record on his first flying lap, then broke it again on his second – going so fast that the commentator didn't report the time because he didn't believe it… With pole position sewn up and the race as good as won, the car then broke a universal joint. Wyer and Parnell were unable to raise anyone at the factory and despaired of the situation, until Wyer's wife phoned to ask how things were going and was rapidly given instructions to get help. Eventually a mechanic came to their rescue by removing an axle from another car at Feltham in the middle of the night, driving up to Liverpool with it, flying to the Isle of Man and then helping to fit it to Parnell's car. After all that, Parnell did the only decent thing he could do – he won the race, by quite some margin…

Parnell won again at Silverstone the following month (heading Salvadori and Collins in an Aston Martin 1-2-3), at Charterhall in August and, with Eric Thompson, at the Goodwood Nine Hours a week later. At the TT the same combination could only manage second to the sister car of Collins and Griffith, the Astons trouncing the Jaguars by being easier on their tyres on the abrasive new surface at Dundrod.

Opposite above Reg Parnell heads for a class win at the B.R.D.C. Silverstone meeting in 1953, in the rebuilt DB3/3.

Opposite below DB3S/6 was one of the Le Mans Coupés, subsequently rebuilt with an open body.

1954 Lagonda V12

Engine:	V12, twin-overhead-cam per bank
Bore/stroke:	82.55mm x 69.85mm
Capacity:	4486cc
Power:	300bhp @ 6000rpm
Fuel system:	4 Weber carburettors
Gearbox:	4-speed David Brown manual
Chassis:	Tubular steel frame
Body:	Aluminium alloy
Suspension:	Front: trailing arms with transverse torsion bars and anti-roll bar. Rear: de Dion with transverse torsion bars
Brakes:	Discs all round
Top speed:	148mph (238km/h)
Acceleration:	0-60mph (97km/h) in 7.5sec (estimated)

For 1954 another new design was being developed. David Brown was keen to build a car to beat the Ferraris in international sports car racing, and for that a bigger engine was needed. Willie Watson came up with a 4.5-litre V12 with many similarities to the LB6 six-cylinder he had designed a decade earlier, including the twin-cam cylinder head and his favourite barrel-type crankcase (also a feature of his previous engines for Invictas and pre-war Lagondas). Unlike the LB6, the Lagonda V12 had a light alloy block, dry-sump lubrication, and 'oversquare' dimensions with an 82.55mm bore and 69.85mm stroke.

Right *David Brown tries the Lagonda at Chalgrove airfield in 1954.*

Lagonda returns to racing

Project 115, the V12 racer, was based on a lengthened DB3S chassis and given a DB3S-style body, but because the new car was to run under the Lagonda banner, the front end was restyled to give the car its own identity. In addition, a supercharged engine was being built for one DB3S, and coupé bodies for two more. The coupé was developed in conjunction with the Vickers aircraft company at Brooklands, the idea being to reduce drag and make the cars quicker down the long Mulsanne straight at Le Mans.

The season did not begin well, with five retirements out of six starts at Buenos Aires and Sebring, then two crashes in the Mille Miglia. For Silverstone three new cars were run – the Lagonda and the two DB3S coupés running as a pre-Le Mans test – with the Lagonda's fifth place in Reg Parnell's hands as the highlight. Then Aston Martin went to Le Mans with an ambitious five-car entry. The plan was for two Lagondas, the two DB3S coupés and the supercharged DB3S to run, but the second Lagonda wasn't ready in time and was replaced by a standard DB3S for Paul Frère and Texan driver Carroll Shelby.

Though the DB3S coupés had less drag than the open cars, they were also very unstable – a common problem with low-drag shapes – and that contributed to their downfall. Both cars crashed just after the hump at White House. The Lagonda had crashed in the Esses early in the race, the standard DB3S broke a stub axle and the supercharged car blew its head gasket. Back at Feltham, the mood was grim.

David Brown was keen to get motor racing again as quickly as possible. The supercharged car was fitted with an unsupercharged engine, the Lagonda and the

Opposite top The unloved Lagonda V12 racer.

Below DB3S Coupé body generated lift which caused both works cars to crash at Le Mans in 1954. This is one of three production cars.

1956 DB3S

Engine:	In-line 6-cylinder, twin-overhead-cam
Bore/stroke:	83mm x 90mm
Capacity:	2922cc
Power:	236bhp @ 6250rpm
Fuel system:	Triple Weber carburettors
Gearbox:	4-speed David Brown manual
Chassis:	Tubular steel frame
Body:	Aluminium alloy
Suspension:	Front: trailing arms with coil springs and anti-roll bar. Rear: coil-sprung live axle located by twin trailing arms
Brakes:	Discs all round
Top speed:	146mph (235km/h)
Acceleration:	0-60mph (97km/h) in 7.5sec (estimated)

Shelby/Frère Le Mans car were repaired, and Wyer fitted the latest-spec twin-plug engine to David Brown's DB3S road car to create a team for Silverstone in July. Morale rocketed when Collins won in the ex-supercharged car, Salvadori was second and Shelby third, with Parnell fourth in the Lagonda. But the up/down season continued: two more crashes marred the TT, though Collins managed second place at Aintree.

Aston Martin diversified into rallying in 1955, entering three DB2/4s for Reg Parnell/Louis Klementaski, Peter Collins/Graham Whitehead and the experienced rallying pair of Maurice Gatsonides/Marcel Becquart, who had won the Monte a couple of years earlier in a Ford Zephyr. Parnell and Collins put themselves out of contention by deciding to get the boring road sections over with as quickly as possible, in the process racking up an enormous number of penalty points for checking into controls early. Gatsonides and Becquart led until Becquart's local knowledge let him down at Annecy, where they passed a secret time-check early and dropped to 70th place. Brilliant driving put them back to seventh, but without that one error they would have won easily. It wasn't all bad news, though: Gatsonides/Becquart won the RAC Trophy for 'comfort and safety', and the preparation of the team was so neat that the organizers created a 'team prize' specially.

Two of the Monte Carlo DB2/4s were entered in the Mille Miglia, along with a lone DB3S for Collins, but none of the cars finished. The big Lagonda, with a new-for-1955 spaceframe chassis to cut weight, had originally been pencilled in for the Mille Miglia but the engine was proving to be a major headache, refusing to hold oil pressure. The problem was with the alloy block, which expanded at the same rate as the alloy bearing carriers so allowing the bearing clearances to open up. The six-cylinder LB6, on which the design was based, worked because it had an iron block which expanded less than the alloy 'cheeses'. The V12, which had been mooted as a future production car engine, was never going to work. When Wyer was promoted to Technical Director in 1955, one of the first decisions he made was to abandon the V12 project. Instead, the focus was switched to a new road car, which would become the DB4, and a new race car with a purpose-built six-cylinder engine to replace the DB3S and the LB6-derived power units.

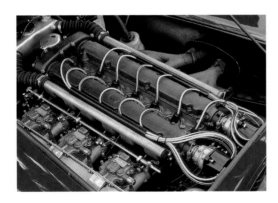

Above Twin-plug head liberated 225bhp.

Right Neither Collins in DB3S/5 nor a pair of DB2/4s finished the 1955 Mille Miglia.

The Competition

Jaguar's challenge in sports car racing mirrored Aston Martin's, as the cars were initially raced in very standard form. For 1951 a tubular-framed competition car, the C-Type or XK120C, appeared and in 1954 Jaguar announced the even more specialized D-Type, with sophisticated aerodynamics by Malcolm Sayer. The XK engine used in all the Jaguars was larger than the Aston unit – usually 3.4-litres, but sometimes 3.8-litres in later years – and that usually gave the Jaguars a speed advantage, though the Astons often handled better.

Mercedes-Benz won Le Mans with its 300SL after the Jaguars failed in 1952, but then withdrew from sports car racing until 1954. The Rudolf Uhlenhaut-designed 300SLR achieved famous victories in 1955, notably at the Mille Miglia with Moss and Denis Jenkinson, but after the Le Mans accident that year the Mercedes team again withdrew.

The Lagonda V12 had been an effort to compete with the Ferrari 375MM and SP, with their Lampredi-designed 60 degree V12s in 4.5-litre and 4.9-litre form developing well over 300bhp. Though these cars were clearly beyond Aston Martin's reach, their engines were outlawed by the 3.0-litre formula of 1958, and Ferrari instead ran the 250 Testa Rossa – again a V12, though this time drawn by Gioacchino Columbo. Still Ferrari had a power advantage, but the Ferraris, like the Jaguars, could never match the Aston's handling.

The mid-engined Porsches were much lighter on their feet, competing with the bigger cars because their lower rate of tyre wear and better fuel consumption enabled them to run in long-distance races with fewer pit stops. And with over 140bhp from its four-cam, 1.5-litre engine, the little Porsche RSK was a serious competitor.

Below Pininfarina-bodied Ferrari 375MM of 1953, well beyond the reach of the DB3S.

Above Moss and Jenkinson in a 300SLR at the Goodwood Festival in 1995.

Left 1953 Le Mans-winning Jaguar C-Type.

Above Collins in DB3S/6 was delayed at the start of the 1955 TT. A virtuoso drive from the back of the field came to nothing when the engine failed.

Below DB3S/9 finished second at Le Mans in 1956 driven by Stirling Moss and Peter Collins.

DB3S improvements

For the one-hour race at Silverstone in May 1955, Aston Martin fielded two new DB3S cars which had modifications to overcome the previous season's problems: beefier, Lagonda-spec final drive units, Girling disc brakes, and the latest twin-plug alloy cylinder heads which helped to boost power substantially, from 190bhp to 225bhp. Parnell and Salvadori used the new cars to good effect, finishing ahead of Mike Hawthorn in the works Jaguar D-Type OKV3, and there was more good news the following day when Paul Frère won at Spa with a DB3S production car. Frère was in the thick of it again at Le Mans, partnering Peter Collins to second place behind the Hawthorn/Bueb D-Type in a race that will always be remembered for the accident which sent Pierre Levegh's Mercedes into the crowd, with horrific results.

The sports car race supporting the British Grand Prix at Aintree a month later was a clean sweep for Aston Martin, Roy Salvadori winning with Collins, Parnell and Peter Walker in line astern – theoretically staying put, on instructions from Wyer, but in reality they were pushing Salvadori every inch of the way…

Salvadori won again at Crystal Palace a couple of weeks later, and the team was successful again in the Goodwood Nine Hours, where Walker and Dennis Poore won in DB3S/7, Salvadori's Aintree car. Parnell blotted his copybook at Goodwood with a fierce getaway which broke a rear hub, but made amends by entering and winning the Oulton Park Gold Cup a week later despite the intimidating presence of Mike Hawthorn in a works Ferrari. After all that, the TT was a relatively undistinguished performance, with

Walker/Poore fourth, and Salvadori/Parnell only seventh. The Peter Collins/Tony Brooks DB3S sadly retired with an engine failure after a virtuoso drive from Collins, recovering from the back of the field after sufffering a starter motor failure when the flag fell.

With the withdrawal of Mercedes-Benz from racing after the Le Mans accident, Stirling Moss joined Aston Martin for 1956. Partnered by Peter Collins he was running second in his first event, at Sebring, when the oil pump drive broke – a fate which also befell the Parnell/Brooks DB3S, leaving Salvadori and Carroll Shelby to salvage some honour for Aston Martin in fourth place. Silverstone in May saw a better result for Moss, second place behind Salvadori, but also some friction between the two of them after a first-lap accident which eliminated Collins, Parnell and the D-Types of Desmond Titterington and Ninian Sanderson.

More decent results were added to the tally, even though work was now in full swing on developing the new car, the DBR1. Salvadori had bought DB3S/5 from the factory and entered it at Spa, but was unable to race because of injury. Parnell took it over, finishing second, and the car was recalled to the works team for Collins and Brooks to race at the Nürburgring 1000km, where they finished fifth despite Collins being off the boil. Moss led three Astons in the top six at Rouen, then finished second and won the class at Le Mans where Brooks and Parnell debuted the new DBR1. Following the 1955 accident the organizers had decreed that 'prototype' cars (where fewer than 50 cars had been made or planned) had to run with 2.5-litre engines, so the DBR1 had to run with a short-stroke 2493cc version of the new RB6 engine – though it gave away only 7bhp to the 2.9-litre unit fitted to the DB3S...

Above Once the works had finished with them, the DB3S team cars were raced privately. This is Moss in DB3S/2 at Mallory Park in 1957.

Below DBR1/4 finished second at Le Mans in 1959, driven by Trintignant and Frère.

1959 DBR1

Engine:	In-line 6-cylinder, twin-overhead-cam
Bore/stroke:	84mm x 90mm
Capacity:	2992cc
Power:	255bhp @ 6000rpm
Fuel system:	3 Weber carburettors
Gearbox:	5-speed David Brown manual
Chassis:	Tubular steel frame
Body:	Aluminium alloy
Suspension:	Front: trailing arms with coil springs and anti-roll bar. Rear: de Dion with transverse torsion bars
Brakes:	Discs all round
Top speed:	158mph (254km/h)
Acceleration:	0-60mph (97km/h) in 6.5sec (estimated)

At Oulton Park in August, Moss again led the Aston Martins home, this time in a 1-2-3-4 finish, and to finish the season Brooks and Salvadori finished first and second at Goodwood. But now all eyes were on the DBR1 for 1957.

The DBR1 and its new engine had been designed by Ted Cutting, who had joined Aston Martin from Allard in 1949. Almost everything was new. The RB6 engine retained the dimensions of the DB3S unit and initially the twin-plug alloy cylinder head was carried over from the old engine. But in place of the Willie Watson 'barrel-type' crankcase, which had been a limitation on the LB6 and the downfall of the V12, Cutting used a conventional light-alloy block with bolted-in main bearing caps. To keep the DBR1's weight to the minimum, a new 'perimeter' spaceframe chassis was constructed, mostly from 1in (25mm) diameter steel tube, and the bodywork mixed 18-gauge and aircraft-spec 20-gauge alloys. The DBR1 weighed in at 195lb (88kg) less than the DB3S.

After second places in Salvadori's hands at Oulton Park and Goodwood early in 1957, all in 2.5-litre form, the DBR1 went to Spa for its first race powered by the 2.9-litre RB6. Brooks won despite some gearbox hiccups, with Salvadori second in another DBR1 and four D-Types giving chase. Brooks won again at the Nürburgring partnered by Noel Cunnigham-Reid, who was in only his second race for Aston Martin – despite his inexperience he increased the lead that the Aston held over the Ferraris and Maseratis during his stint, and the car won by more than four minutes. Meanwhile, the sister car of Salvadori and Les Leston finished sixth, after being stuck in fourth gear for the last eight laps of the race.

Right Cockpit of DBR1/3, the car Moss used to attack the Ferraris at Le Mans in 1959. Note the multitude of small-diameter tubes, which form the car's spaceframe chassis.

Transmission troubles reappeared at Le Mans, where the race regulations reverted to the no-holds-barred 1955 rules. Aston Martin entered three cars, the two DBR1s from the Nürburgring 1000km (both cars with the same driver pairing as in the German race – Salvadori/Leston and Brooks/Cunningham-Reid) and a new car, the DBR2, to be driven by Graham and Peter Whitehead. The DBR2 combined the Lagonda spaceframe chassis with an experimental 3.7-litre (later 3.9 litre) engine – the Tadek Marek-designed unit destined for the DB4. The DBR2 went out when the gearbox breather became blocked and the box lost all its oil; Brooks crashed his DBR1 while trying to find a gear and the other Aston was retired, locked in fourth gear.

Brooks was back in the same car, DBR1/2, at Spa for the Belgian GP, which was for sports cars that year. After a scare in practice when the engine lost oil pressure and destroyed its crankshaft (David Brown flew out a replacement in his De Havilland Dove), Brooks won the race, keeping a close eye on the oil pressure all the way. To finish the season, Salvadori in the DBR2 beat Archie Scott-Brown's Lister-Jaguar at Silverstone, with Cunningham-Reid's DBR2 in third and Brooks fourth in his regular DBR1.

More regulation changes for 1958 limited the cars to 3.0-litres, ideal for the DBR1. Moss rejoined the team, partnering Tony Brooks in DBR1/2 at Sebring, but the car went out with more gearbox trouble. Salvadori and Shelby in DBR1/1, the original prototype DBR1, retired with a broken chassis – the prototype never having been updated to the stronger design of the later cars.

Moss and Brooks picked up some good results in British events in the DBR2s that spring, though they couldn't beat the Lister-Jaguars at Silverstone in May where Moss gave the DBR3 its only run. This was a DBR1 fitted with a 2990cc version of the DB4 engine, which seized before the end of the race. The car was subsequently converted to normal DBR1 spec.

Above Though it looked similar to the DBR1, the DBR2 had a different chassis (derived from the V12 Lagonda's) and a larger engine.

Below Not eligible for World Championship racing, the DBR2 (here seen in Tony Brooks' hands) was still effective in British events.

1957 DBR2

Engine:	In-line 6-cylinder, twin-overhead-cam
Bore/stroke:	95mm x 92mm
Capacity:	3910cc
Power:	300bhp @ 5800rpm
Fuel system:	3 Weber carburettors
Gearbox:	5-speed David Brown manual
Chassis:	Tubular steel frame
Body:	Aluminium alloy
Suspension:	Front: trailing arms with transverse torsion bars and anti-roll bar. Rear: de Dion with transverse torsion bars
Brakes:	Discs all round
Top speed:	164mph (264km/h)
Acceleration:	0-60mph (97km/h) in 6.0sec (estimated)

A third DBR1 chassis was built up for the Targa Florio, where Moss was quick but the transmission again failed. At the Nürburgring 1000km he shared the same car with a new recruit, Jack Brabham, driving hard for 36 of the 44 laps and winning the race by almost four minutes from the Hawthorn/Collins Ferrari Testa Rossa. The other two DBR1s didn't fare so well: Brooks was forced off the road by a slower car on his penultimate lap, Salvadori's gearbox expired, and both cars retired.

Another gearbox failure put Brooks and Maurice Trintignant out at Le Mans, where DBR1/2 lasted longer than its team-mates. Moss had led easily for 30 laps until the engine failed in DBR1/3, while Stuart Lewis-Evans crashed the prototype DBR1 in the rain on lap 48. There was some consolation in a 1-2-3 finish at the Goodwood Tourist Trophy, but by then Ferrari had wrapped up the World Championship and so they didn't enter the TT. A season that had seemed made for the DBR1 had not gone Aston Martin's way.

For 1959 the plan was to field the DBR1s only at Le Mans but the Sebring organizers pleaded with Astons to enter, so the 'spare' DBR1/1 was sent for Salvadori and Shelby to race. It retired with clutch failure. Then Moss asked if he could take it to the Nürburgring, where again he did the lion's share of the driving. Jack Fairman's first stint ended prematurely when he was forced off the road and into a ditch, Fairman heaving the car back onto the track for Moss to take over, and the pair went on to win Aston's third successive 1000km. Two weeks later came the assault on Le Mans.

Moss was again paired with Jack Fairman in DBR1/3, his 1958 Le Mans car. Salvadori partnered Shelby in DBR1/2, which had given Brooks four wins during 1957/58. Two new DBR1s appeared, a works car for Trintignant/Frère and a private entry for Whitehead/Naylor. Wind-tunnel work had led to the cars being given shrouded wheel arches and a higher tail, but most of the development time had been concentrated on making the cars more reliable.

Right The 1958 Le Mans did not go to plan for Aston Martin: number 2 (Moss/Brabham) broke a conrod, number 3 (Brooks/Trintignant) broke its gearbox and number 4 (Shelby/Lewis-Evans) crashed.

Attacking Ferrari

The three works cars were assigned very different game plans. The Ferraris were known to be fast, but fragile in hot weather, so Moss was to attack them early on, forcing the pace to work the three Ferraris hard. Salvadori would run comfortable 4min 20sec laps to preserve the car, while Trintignant would lap at a cautious 4min 22sec to act as a reserve. To that end DBR1/3 was given a more powerful four-bearing version of the RB6, while the other two cars had the tougher seven-bearing engine.

Aston Martin drew first blood, Moss lapping at an average of 4min 13sec during the early part of the race – astonishingly fast given that the best DBR1 practice laps had been 4min 11sec – to take an early lead. Even so, the Jean Behra/Dan Gurney Ferrari overhauled the Aston to lead into the evening. Honours even. The number 15 Ferrari of 'Nano' da Silva Ramos and Cliff Allison retired after just 41 laps with gearbox trouble, but then Jack Fairman brought in DBR1/3 with fluctuating oil pressure – despite a couple more slow laps, it was all over for the Moss/Fairman car. As night fell Shelby led in DBR1/2, from the third works Ferrari of 1958 winners Olivier Gendebien and Phil Hill. More gearbox trouble claimed the Behra/Gurney Ferrari after 10 hours, but it was the Gendebien/Hill Ferrari that led through the night.

Salvadori brought the leading Aston into the pits early on Sunday morning reporting a vibration: when he finished his stint half an hour later, it was found that one of the rear Avons had thrown its tread. Meanwhile, the Trintignant/Frère Aston moved slowly up the lap chart to third, maintaining the planned lap times despite Trintignant suffering from a blistered foot, caused by the DBR1's new under-floor exhaust. Then, just after 11am, Gendebien pulled the lead Ferrari into the pits – the head gasket was failing. The Ferrari challenge was over.

Reg Parnell, who had taken over from John Wyer as team manager, signalled to Salvadori to reduce the pace. Paul Frère took over DBR1/4 at 1.45pm, Shelby replaced Salvadori in DBR1/2 20 minutes later, and from there it was an easy run to the finish. Salvadori and Shelby won, cheered on from the Aston pit by Moss and young British driver Innes Ireland, with Trintignant and Frère just a lap behind. Aston Martin had finally won at Le Mans.

The win meant that just a few points separated Ferrari, Porsche and Aston Martin in the World Sports Car Championship, with only the Tourist Trophy left to run. Aston Martin sent the three Le Mans DBR1s to Goodwood, pairing Moss with Salvadori in DBR1/3, Shelby and Fairman in DBR1/2 and Trintignant/Frère in their usual DBR1/4. Goodwood was known to be heavy on tyres, necessitating pit stops for fresh rubber every 75 minutes or so. To speed up the pit stops, all three cars were fitted with on-board jacks, activated by compressed nitrogen supplied from a bottle in the pit garage.

Moss and Salvadori led easily until Roy came in for a fuel and tyre stop on lap 94. Somehow the lever on the refuelling hose was knocked on, spilling fuel over the back of the car. In moments the car and the wooden pit garage were ablaze; Salvadori leapt out over the bonnet, escaping with burns to his hands and face. Graham Whitehead withdrew his own DBR1 to give the works team the use of his pit and Moss took over the second-placed Shelby/Fairman car for the rest of the race to win by a lap from the Jo Bonnier/Wolfgang von Trips Porsche. Aston Martin were the World Champions.

Above Aston Martin finally won at Le Mans in 1959. Carroll Shelby shared the winning DBR1 with Roy Salvadori, seen here early in the race.

The Englishman's Ferrari

Fast, elegant and well-made, the DB2 and its derivatives had proved to be the most popular Aston Martins yet, but by 1954 work was under way to create a successor. Unlike the DB2, the car that would be the result of this work would owe nothing to Claude Hill's wartime Atom – but nor would it owe anything to W.O. Bentley's Lagondas. This would be a completely new design, with a brand new engine, ready to take Aston Martin into the 1960s.

Londoner Harold Beach had joined Aston Martin as a draughtsman in 1950, after a varied early career which included spells with the Barker coachbuilding company and work on commercial and military vehicles. While Tadek Marek started planning a new engine design, Beach laid out a new perimeter-frame chassis with wishbone front suspension, instead of the DB2's trailing links, and a de Dion axle at the rear to replace the old trailing arms. Development Project 114, as the car was known, was fitted with a 2.9-litre DB2 engine and a simple test body, in which form it racked up many thousands of test miles. It was later fitted with a four-seater Frank Feeley body and used by David Brown and his wife.

But DP114 would not become the basis for the new car, even though everyone at the time called it 'the DB4' – at least, they did when they weren't calling it the 'Wall's ice cream van', a reference to its two-tone white and blue paintwork. John Wyer had decided that the new Aston Martin's body should be styled by Touring of Milan, and built on their *Superleggera* principle – similar in concept to Claude Hill's tubular body structure for the Atom 15 years earlier. The relationship between Touring and Aston Martin began well with three open 'spyders' based on DB2/4 Mark II chassis in 1956, the first of them being given away as a prize in a *Daily Mail* competition during the 1956 Motor Show. Sadly, Touring's plans for a short production run came to nothing.

Beach was despatched to Milan to work on the body for the DB4, but found Touring unwilling to use the perimeter frame he had designed. Instead, they proposed a platform chassis welded together from small steel panels, with a tubular body frame welded to it and providing extra stiffness and strength. Beach could see the advantages of Touring's

Above An early first series DB4. The bonnet scoop and bumpers were soon changed.

Previous page 1962 DB4.

Right DP114/2, seen at the Goodwood Festival in 1996. Originally blue and white, it was nicknamed 'the Wall's ice cream van'.

proposal – the whole car could be both lighter and stiffer, as the Atom had proved – and he set about designing a platform chassis to use the DP114 suspension. Initially the production chassis would be built at Farsley in Yorkshire (at the David Brown tractor factory) and then sent to Astons for the body to be built, using the Touring *Superleggera* system under licence.

Beach worked closely with Marek, who had already redesigned the Bentley/Watson 3.0-litre engine to produce the DBA, and was now working on the replacement. Wyer's idea for DP186, as the new engine was known, was an all-alloy, 3.0-litre six with the potential for expansion to 3.5-litres, but for a road car engine Marek preferred to stay with a more conventional and conservative iron block. To offset the extra weight and provide power without the need for a high-stressed engine, he opted for a larger capacity of 3670cc. Now that British manufacturers were finally rid of the absurd 'RAC horsepower' taxation formula, which taxed a car based on its cylinder bore, more modern dimensions with a bigger bore and shorter stroke were used. DP186 in fact was 'square', with both bore and stroke set at 92mm. As with the DBA, there was an alloy cylinder head with hemispherical combustion chambers, central spark plugs and angled valves operated by twin chain-driven overhead camshafts. The distributor was driven from the inlet-side camshaft and sat at the back of the engine between the cam covers.

Above Touring of Milan built three of these DB2/4 Mark II Spyders, then styled the DB4.

Above John Wyer, in characteristic pose.

Right This unique DB4GT carries a (steel) body designed by the 20-year-old Giorgetto Giugiaro for Bertone.

1958 DB4

Engine:	In-line 6-cylinder, twin-overhead-cam
Bore/stroke:	92mm x 92mm
Capacity:	3670cc
Power:	240bhp @ 5500rpm
Fuel system:	Twin SU carburettors
Gearbox:	4-speed David Brown manual
Chassis:	Steel platform
Body:	Tubular steel body frame with aluminium alloy panels
Suspension:	Front: wishbones with coil springs and anti-roll bar. Rear: coil-sprung live axle located by twin trailing arms and Watt linkage
Brakes:	Dunlop discs all round, servo assisted
Top speed:	140mph (225km/h)
Acceleration:	0-60mph (97km/h) in 9sec

Developing the DB4

DP186 didn't keep its iron cylinder block for long. With Britain's motor industry now getting going again in earnest after the war, Aston Martin couldn't find a foundry with enough capacity to cast the blocks, though spare capacity was available for aluminium alloy blocks. So DP186 was given an alloy block after all, with Marek hastily redesigning it for the fitment of iron cylinder liners. In this form it made its public debut in the DBR2 racing car at Le Mans in June 1957 – much against the wishes of Marek, who wasn't at all sure that the alloy motor was up to the rigours of racing, having only ever envisaged it as a road car engine. He need not have worried: though Graham and Peter Whitehead retired the car after 81 laps, it was gearbox trouble that put them out, not problems with the engine. Roy Salvadori would go on to record the DBR2's first win at Silverstone late in 1957, where the extra power of the 3.7-litre unit (developing nearly 280bhp in race spec) finally gave him the edge over Archie Scott-Brown's 3.8-litre Lister-Jaguar.

Beach's suspension had been proven on DP114, while Marek's engine (developing 240bhp in road trim) went into a DB2/4 Mark II for testing. The engine and suspension were brought together, along with Beach's platform chassis and Touring's styling, on DP184/1 – the prototype DB4, which was running in the summer of 1957. David Brown was the first person to drive it in anger, just a couple of days after it was finished, and he described it as 'very promising' to Beach and Wyer. Even so, changes would be made before the car reached production: the de Dion rear suspension had to be dropped because it allowed too much transmission noise to reach the interior. As the transmission could not be quietened (ironic given that the David Brown company made its name in gears), the rear suspension was replaced by a more conventional coil-sprung live axle, located longitudinally by radius arms and transversely by a Watt linkage. At the front, Beach's unequal-length double wishbone layout was retained, again using coil springs (with Armstrong telescopic dampers inside them) and fitted with an anti-roll bar. Dunlop disc brakes were fitted all round.

Although shown to the public at the London Motor Show of 1958, the DB4 was not fully developed by then. The switch from iron to alloy for the cylinder block resulted in

lubrication problems, the bearing clearances changing as the engine warmed up just as they had on the Lagonda V12 and, to some extent, the LB6. Marek arranged for high oil pressure, but the engine needed a bigger volume of oil, an oil cooler and lots of work on the bottom end before it was a reliable proposition, none of which it received before production began.

Above *The DB4 evolved through five major phases during its production run. This is a 'Series 3'.*

As fast as Ferrari

1959 DB4GT

Engine:	In-line 6-cylinder, twin-overhead-cam
Bore/stroke:	92mm x 92mm
Capacity:	3670cc
Power:	302bhp @ 6000rpm
Fuel system:	Triple Weber carburettors
Gearbox:	4-speed David Brown manual
Chassis:	Steel platform
Body:	Tubular steel body frame with aluminium alloy panels
Suspension:	Front: wishbones with coil springs and anti-roll bar. Rear: coil-sprung live axle located by twin trailing arms and Watt linkage
Brakes:	Girling discs all round
Top speed:	145mph est (233km/h)
Acceleration:	0-60mph (97km/h) in 6.5sec

Public and press reaction to the new Aston Martin was overwhelmingly positive. The company claimed that the DB4 could accelerate from rest to 100mph (161km/h) and brake to a standstill in under half a minute, and it was no idle boast – the car was easily capable of it. So here was a British grand touring car which was as fast as a Ferrari, as good looking as a Ferrari thanks to Touring's Italianate styling, better built than any Italian exotic, and with enough space for four people, as long as they were friends. It was hardly a cheap car, but at two-thirds the price of a Ferrari, it left you enough change to buy a trendy new Mini…

It took the magazines a while to get their hands on a car to test: *Road & Track* beat the others to it with a road test in 1959, but that had been written by a certain Roy Salvadori… The British journal *The Motor* had to wait until 1960, and its rival *Autocar* until 1961 and by then several changes had been made to the DB4. Chrome window surrounds and bigger bumpers with over-riders were added after the first 50 cars had been built, then early in 1960 a 'Series 2' specification was phased in, with a front-hinged bonnet and a much-needed increase in sump capacity (up from 15 pints to 17 [8.5 to 9.7lit], and increased again the following year to 21 pints [11.9lit]). An oil cooler was now an optional extra, though one that surprisingly few owners took advantage of. Electric windows and overdrive were also available.

By this time a racing derivative of the DB4 had also been announced. Apart from its cowled headlamps and smoother nose, the DB4GT looked very similar to the DB4, but close inspection revealed that the rear seats had gone, replaced by a carpeted luggage area.

Aston Martin's Grand Prix Cars

Grand Prix racing attracted Aston Martin's attention as far back as 1951, though early attempts to piece together a car to 'have a go' were quashed by Chief Engineer Eberan von Eberhorst: always insistent on approaching everything from first principles, he wouldn't hear of such a 'bitsa' approach…

A single-seater based on the DB3S was built in 1955 for Reg Parnell to race in New Zealand, but serious work on a Grand Prix car did not begin until 1956, at the same time as the DBR1 sports car. The DBR4, as the car was called, was built up around a DBR1-style spaceframe chassis with wishbone front suspension – originally using longitudinal torsion bars, but later fitted with coil springs and DB4 suspension arms. At the back there was a three-piece de Dion tube located by a Watt linkage. Power came from a short-stroke 2.5-litre version of the RB6 engine.

The DBR4 was tested at the end of 1957 and ready to run in 1958. But with changes to the sports car race regulations that year outlawing the larger-engined competition, Aston Martin felt their time had finally come and they decided to concentrate on sports car racing. The DBR4 spent most of 1958 sitting under a dust sheet.

So the car did not make its debut until the International Trophy at Silverstone 1959, where Salvadori finished an encouraging second to Jack Brabham's

Cooper and broke the lap record. But the Cooper was the shape of things to come: the rear-engined revolution was sweeping Formula One racing and the big front-engined cars were out of date. Brabham would win the World Championship that year, and the next, in the rear-engined Coopers, and soon the results sheets would be chock full of rear-engined Lotuses, BRMs – and then Ferraris. Had the DBR4 raced in 1958 it would have been very competitive, but allowing it to sit idle for a year had rendered it obsolete.

For 1960 another new front-engined car was built, despite the writing on the wall. The DBR5 was much smaller and lighter, in an attempt to compete with the toy-like Coopers and Lotuses. It didn't work. Further lightening was attempted, and independent rear suspension was tried, but the cars were too far behind the times. By the middle of 1960 Wyer and Brown could see that, and the project was cancelled.

Perhaps the most telling comment on the Grand Prix cars came from Stirling Moss, when he drove a rebuilt DBR4 for the first time at Goodwood in 1980. Moss – who, remember, drove front-engined Maserati, Mercedes and Vanwall Grand Prix cars and rear-engined Coopers and Lotuses – was surprised at the DBR4's speed, saying 'I'd no idea it was as good as it is'. If only…

Five inches (127mm) had been taken out of the wheelbase and overall length, making the GT easier to handle on a race track and reducing the overall weight slightly. It had Girling brakes and Borrani wire wheels in place of the DB4's Dunlop items, and at the back the Salisbury final drive gained a 'Powr-Lok' limited-slip differential. A 30-gallon (136lit) fuel tank sat under the spare wheel, between them almost filling the boot. Though the engine capacity remained at 3670cc the engine gained a second distributor driven off the exhaust camshaft and six more spark plugs, the DB4's twin SU carburettors were replaced by three Weber 45DCOEs, and the compression ratio was raised from 8.25:1 to 9:1. Bigger inlet

Above Roy Salvadori at Zandvoort in 1959. *The DBR4 lasted just four laps.*

Opposite DB4GT *was handsome and effective.*

Above The twin-plug engine of the DB4GT also powered the 'Project' cars – this is DP215.

valves were controlled by a higher lift camshaft and, sensibly, an oil cooler was standard fitment. Output jumped from the DB4's 240bhp to a claimed 302bhp, and the 0-100mph (161km/h) time was slashed from the DB4's already very swift 21 seconds to a shatteringly fast 15 seconds.

This time Aston Martin claimed that the DB4GT could despatch the 0-100-0 test in less than 20 seconds, a claim that was received sceptically in some areas – but the car could do it, and Reg Parnell went out and proved it. Working the watches beside him was Des O'Dell, at the time Aston Martin's 'Mr Fixit'. He was later to achieve success as the Rootes Group's competitions manager.

The prototype DB4GT made its racing debut in the hands of Stirling Moss at Silverstone in May 1959, winning the race and setting a new 'GT class' lap record in the process. It was also entered at Le Mans in June by 'Equipe Trois Chevrons', though that wasn't such a success. Running in the prototype class, it had to be fitted with a 3.0-litre engine, and that was the short-stroke (92x75mm) unit that had powered the DBR3 on its one appearance in 1958. As on that occasion the engine again destroyed a bearing and the car was eliminated early on. Aston Martin's works team withdrew from sports car racing after the Le Mans and World Championship success of 1959, and concentrated on its ill-fated Grand Prix car project. It was left to privateer teams to uphold Aston Martin honour on the racetracks with the DB4GT, the best of them – such as John Ogier's Essex Racing Stable – receiving a measure of works support. At least five lightweight cars – even lighter than normal – were built, the first three of them for Ogier.

Enter the Zagato

By 1960 the Essex Racing Stable and others were armed with Aston Martin's next weapon in the fight against the Ferraris. Like Touring, Zagato was a Milanese coachbuilder, and they had a reputation for designs that were eye-catching, though not always because of their beauty. But the design that their young stylist Ercole Spada came up with for the DB4GT was one of their best, and one of anyone's best. It managed to look like an Aston

Right The prototype DB4GT, restored to look exactly as it did when Hubert Patthey and Jacques Calderari raced it at Le Mans in 1959.

Opposite above Innes Ireland looks on as new wheels are fitted to his Essex Racing Stable DB4GT during the 1961 Fordwater Trophy at Goodwood. Note the Zagato in the background, driven by Stirling Moss.

Opposite below One of 19 DB4GT Zagatos.

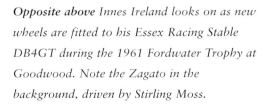

1960 DB4GT Zagato

Engine:	In-line 6-cylinder, twin-overhead-cam
Bore/stroke:	92mm x 92mm
Capacity:	3670cc
Power:	314bhp @ 6000rpm
Fuel system:	Triple Weber carburettors
Gearbox:	4-speed David Brown manual
Chassis:	Steel platform
Body:	Tubular steel body frame with aluminium alloy panels
Suspension:	Front: wishbones with coil springs and anti-roll bar. Rear: coil-sprung live axle located by twin trailing arms and Watt linkage
Brakes:	Girling discs all round
Top speed:	150mph (242km/h)
Acceleration:	0-60mph (97km/h) in 6.2sec

Martin, while at the same time blending in an extra dose of purpose and aggression compared to the subtler Touring shape. It proved to be a very influential design, and one that would reappear in several forms in later Aston Martins.

Though the regular DB4 and DB4GT were assembled entirely in Britain, the Zagato's production process was more expensive and more long-winded. Complete DB4GT chassis were shipped to Milan, where Zagato built the bodies. These were constructed using beaten aluminium panels, the standard method for hand-built bodies and the kind of thing

Above Each one of the Zagatos was subtly different to the rest. This car, with DB4-style exposed headlights, is the most individual.

Below Jim Clark fights one of the John Ogier Zagatos at Goodwood. He called the Aston a 'big heavy beast'.

you would see on a contemporary Ferrari. Aston Martin had always used 'wheeled' panels, where the basic shape of panel is created by bending and stretching the aluminium with a pair of closely-set wheels, rather than beating the panel with hammers. Normally the cars were then returned from Zagato to Aston Martin for trimming, though five were in fact finished in Italy.

The result was a slightly lighter car (though much of the gain was made by fitting plastic windows and even less trim than on the DB4GT, and deleting the bumpers) and with a higher compression ratio it produced more power, a claimed 314bhp. It cost more, too, thanks to the cost of shipping chassis and cars to Italy and back. In 1961 a standard DB4 could have been yours for a fraction less than £4000, and a DB4GT would have set you back £4668; the Zagato was a colossal £5470.

Just 19 Zagatos were built (all of them, happily, still exist). One had a DB4-style front end without the headlamps cowls, and occasional rear seats, and there are detail differences between the other cars. Probably the most famous of them are the Essex Racing Stable pair registered 1VEV and 2VEV. At the 1961 Goodwood TT these cars and Ogier's lightweight DB4GT won the team prize in the hands of Salvadori, a young Jimmy Clark and Innes Ireland. It was Clark's first race in the Zagato, a car he later described as a 'big heavy beast to drive'. The following year at the same race, in the same car, the point was proved: Clark couldn't keep up with the Ferrari 250GTOs, and then when race leader John Surtees came by to lap him, the Aston got away from him around the bumpy Madgwick Corner and both cars spun out of the race. Jimmy was very apologetic, but Surtees just said, 'Well, that's motor racing'.

Production of the DB4GT and Zagato ended in 1962, by which time Aston Martin's dealers were putting pressure on the company to get back into competition – and specifically Le Mans – with a works team. A single car, DP212, was hurriedly built for the 1962 race to test the water. Based on a production platform chassis, it had a very light, low-drag coupé body, and a DB4GT engine linered out to give a 96mm bore and a capacity of 3995cc – an idea pioneered on the DBR2 in 1958. Modified DB4 wishbones were used at the front, with a de Dion axle at the back. BRM Grand Prix drivers Graham Hill and Richie Ginther drove it, once they'd worked out how to get them both to fit it, as Hill was a six-footer and Ginther a lithe five feet three inches. The Californian had a special removable seat which fitted inside Hill's. In practice, the drivers found rear end lift made the car skittish in fast corners and Ginther – using his Ferrari testing experience – suggested that a rear spoiler might help. Hill made a superb start and led the first lap by

1963 DP214	
Engine:	In-line 6-cylinder, twin-overhead-cam
Bore/stroke:	93mm x 92mm
Capacity:	3750cc
Power:	317bhp @ 6000rpm
Fuel system:	Triple Weber carburettors
Gearbox:	4-speed David Brown manual
Chassis:	Steel box-section
Body:	Tubular steel body frame with aluminium alloy panels
Suspension:	Front: wishbones with coil springs and anti-roll bar. Rear: coil-sprung live axle located by twin trailing arms and Watt linkage
Brakes:	Girling discs all round
Top speed:	186mph (300km/h)
Acceleration:	0-60mph (97km/h) in 6.5sec (estimated)

Left Mike Salmon lines up DP212 on the startline at the Goodwood Festival in 1994.

Left The Kimberley/Schlesser DP214 being worked on prior to Le Mans 1963 in the courtyard at the Hotel de France in La Chartre – Aston Martin's traditional Le Mans headquarters.

Reinventing Lagonda: the Rapide

Production of the 3.0-litre Lagonda saloons, based on W.O. Bentley's wartime design, had ended in February 1958. Effectively the hand-built Lagondas had been killed off by the startling competence and value for money of the monocoque Jaguar 3.4 of 1957. Though the Jaguar couldn't compete with the Lagonda's build quality, it was more than a match in terms of performance, and that's what counted for most buyers. But David Brown was keen to keep the Lagonda marque alive, and in 1961 a new model was announced.

The Rapide was based on the DB4's steel platform chassis, but lengthened by 16in (406mm) to provide more rear leg-room and space for four doors. The front suspension was by DB4 coil springs and wishbones, while the rear suspension used a de Dion arrangement – just as Harold Beach had proposed for the DB4 in 1952. Fabricated trailing arms located the wheels fore and aft, while the de Dion tube was located laterally by a Watt linkage and springing was by transverse torsion bars. The brakes, Dunlop discs as on the DB4, were mounted outboard at the rear. The standard engine was a DB4-derived 4.0-litre unit, two years before the larger capacity engine would appear in the DB5. The greater capacity was intended to afford the Lagonda greater flexibility, and to this end it was fitted with two Solex twin-choke carbs rather than the triple SUs that would grace the DB5. It was an odd choice as it provided four carburettor throats for six cylinders, making the engine difficult to tune properly as a result. A DB4 'Special Series' engine was offered as an alternative. A 3-speed Borg Warner automatic transmission was fitted as standard, with a manual gearbox available as an option.

All of which was fine. The Lagonda's

real problem – apart from the Mk2 Jaguar 3.8 introduced in 1959, which was less than half the price and even better than its predecessor – was its styling. The body was constructed using the tubular-frame *Superleggera* method, like the DB4, and Touring styled it to look like a longer, four-door DB4. By the time it reached production it had been modified with a front end that combined elements of the old Lagonda V12 racer's original three-nostril nose with all the grace and flair of Ford's famously unsuccessful Edsel. The desire to make the Lagonda clearly different in looks to the Aston Martins, and to give it styling that would appeal in the American market, had resulted in a curious blend of themes that didn't really gel together.

Just 55 cars were sold before the plug was pulled on Lagonda production in 1964 and today that makes the Rapide a rare and, in some ways, charming period piece. If you can get used to the styling, then you have a 4.0-litre sporting saloon built with Lagonda quality and which corners the way Harold Beach had originally intended, thanks to its de Dion rear end.

After the Rapide's demise, the Lagonda marque would not reappear at all until 1971, and then only briefly. Lagonda would not be revived in earnest until the mid-1970s.

Below Unhappy styling marred Lagonda's early-1960s revival, the Rapide.

1961 Lagonda Rapide

Engine:	In-line 6-cylinder, twin-overhead-cam
Bore/stroke:	96mm x 92mm
Capacity:	3995cc
Power:	236bhp @ 5000rpm
Fuel system:	Twin Solex carburettors
Gearbox:	Borg Warner automatic
Chassis:	Steel platform
Body:	Tubular steel body frame with aluminium alloy panels
Suspension:	Front: wishbones with coil springs and anti-roll bar. Rear: de Dion with transverse torsion bars and radius arms
Brakes:	Discs all round
Top speed:	130mph (209km/h) estimated
Acceleration:	0-60mph (97km/h) in 9.0sec (estimated)

almost the length of the pits straight. Wyer commented that if you can't win you must make fastest lap, and if you can't do that, you should lead at end of lap 1. Unfortunately, that's all DP212 could do, as it retired after six hours when a piston failed.

More 'Project' cars

Three more cars were built for 1963, two DP214 cars to run in the production class as 'modified DB4GTs' and a more radical DP215 for the prototype class. All three used very light box-section frames instead of the production-based platform chassis, which effectively made the DP214s illegal. Both DP214s ran with 3.7-litre engines, theoretically the same as the production DB4GT, though a loophole was found which allowed them to be bored out to 93mm to get 3750cc and produce 317bhp. They were mounted further back than in DP212, to improve weight distribution. DP215 had a dry-sumped, 96x92mm 4.0-litre engine developing 323bhp, and it was designed to be capable of using the V8 engine that was on Tadek Marek's drawing board. It also featured double-wishbone independent rear suspension with a wide-based lower wishbone, another idea that was intended to pave the way for future production Astons. Wind-tunnel work at the Motor Industry Research Association over the winter had shown that DP212 developed more than 500lb (227kg) of lift at the back at 175mph (282km/h), so all three new cars sported a rear spoiler, just as Richie Ginther had suggested in 1962!

The DP214s proved to be extremely quick at the Le Mans test day, being the first cars officially clocked at over 300km/h (186mph) on the long Mulsanne straight. DP215 wasn't ready for the test, but when it got to Le Mans it proved even quicker: Phil Hill was timed at 198.6mph (319.6km/h) along the straight. The car's designer, Ted Cutting, believed that the timing strip was too early on the straight and that they actually went even quicker before braking for the tight Mulsanne corner.

Above left DP215 was the last of the David Brown-era works Astons.

Above DP215's interior: note the lightweight drilled pedals.

Right Le Mans 1963: the Hill/Bianchi DP215 (car 18) and McLaren/Ireland DP214 (8) are split by the Rodriquez/Penske Ferrari (10).

Above A year later, Mike Salmon and Peter Sutcliffe ran DP214 at Le Mans as a private entry. It retired in the 18th hour.

Though they were fast, none of the three Astons proved able to last the race. Phil Hill and Lucien Bianchi in DP215 retired after just 29 laps when the transmission failed – it was a David Brown transaxle, just the same as the ones that had given so much trouble in the less-powerful DBR1. Both DP214s retired with broken pistons, Bruce McLaren/Innes Ireland after 50 laps, and Bill Kimberley/Jo Schlesser after 146. Cast pistons had been used, because the correct forged pistons could not be supplied in time.

With the DP214s out of action, DP215 ran again at a sports car race supporting the French GP at Reims, where Jo Schlesser encountered more aerodynamic problems at high speed. But again the gearbox proved its downfall. Schlesser struggled to find gears and as a result bent a valve. The 214s reappeared at the Tourist Trophy in the hands of Innes Ireland and Bruce McLaren, where in practice they proved that they could equal the best Ferrari GTO lap times. But for the race the scrutineers decreed that the cars had to run on 5.5in-wide wheels, because that was the size stated on the homologation papers for the DB4GT. Since then the cars had been upgraded to 6.5in rims, as had all the production cars, and the track measurement quoted assumed that 6.5in wheels were fitted – with 5.5in wheels, the track would not match the homologated spec. On top of that, the cars had run with the wider wheels at Le Mans without query. None of that impressed the scrutineers, who demanded 5.5in wheels. This added more than half a second to the Astons' lap times and put them out of contention. As Ireland pointed out later, the Astons were still illegal in the form they raced because the track was wrong, so why not let them race in a condition where they could put on a spectacle for the crowd? At the green flag Graham Hill in a GTO disappeared into the distance, while McLaren retired from the race with a bent valve. Ireland certainly did provide a spectacle, though not in the way he would have preferred: starting from pole position he finished seventh after driving like a man possessed. Much of his race was spent going sideways and duelling manfully with the GTO of Mike Parkes. The pair went through the Goodwood chicane side by side on more than one lap.

Final victory

The last appearance of the 214s as full works entries was at the Coppa Inter-Europa at Monza, Ferrari territory, where Bianchi and Salvadori took on that man Mike Parkes in another GTO. All through the race the crowd were right behind Salvadori, because they thought he was Italian; Englishman Parkes got a cool reception, despite driving a Ferrari. Salvadori and Parkes were closely matched during the first half of the race; swift pit-work gave Salvadori the edge after the fuel and tyre stop at half distance, and the two cars swapped places almost every lap from there to the end of the three-hour race, Salvadori finally pulling out a few yards to win. A loose sump baffle gave Bianchi oil pressure worries in the other DP214, but even so he managed to stay in front of David Piper in another GTO to take third place.

The 214s had a brief but eventful works career, and then passed to private entrants. Aston Martin's French distributor Marcel Blondeau entered them in French events, recording two more wins. DP214/1 raced on in the hands of Salvadori, Mike Salmon and others, but DP214/2 was wrecked when Brian Hetreed crashed at the Nürburgring in 1964. Hetreed died from his injuries, and the car was returned to Britain and scrapped. A car bearing that identity popped up in the 1990s, but it proved to have been made up – very nicely – from parts which had no connection with the original car: it was effectively a replica of the scrapped DP214/2.

While the Aston Martin name was kept in the limelight on the race tracks, specification changes continually appeared to improve the production DB4 and to make sure it was always big news at any motor show. New rear lights had been fitted to the Series 3 of April 1961, and a 'Special Series' engine option was offered: three SU carburettors instead of two, 9:1 compression ratio instead of 8.25:1, and bigger valves. It was half way to a DB4GT engine, though without the twin-choke Webers and the twin-plug ignition. Its claimed power output of 266bhp was up 26bhp on the standard DB4. Most cars with Special Series engines were also fitted with the DB4GT-style front end with the cowled headlights, in which form the car was known as the DB4 Vantage, but the engine was available without the styling changes as a £125 option. The twin-ignition GT engine was also offered in the DB4 body, though only a dozen or so 'DB4 Vantage GTs' were built.

Left A convertible DB4 was announced at the London Motor Show in 1961. This left-hand-drive example dates from 1963.

1963 DB5

Engine:	In-line 6-cylinder, twin-overhead-cam
Bore/stroke:	96mm x 92mm
Capacity:	3995cc
Power:	282bhp @ 5500rpm
Fuel system:	Triple SU carburettors
Gearbox:	5-speed ZF manual
Chassis:	Steel platform
Body:	Tubular steel body frame with aluminium alloy panels
Suspension:	Front: wishbones with coil springs and anti-roll bar. Rear: coil-sprung live axle located by twin trailing arms and Watt linkage
Brakes:	Girling discs all round, servo assisted
Top speed:	143mph (230km/h)
Acceleration:	0-60mph (97km/h) in 7.4sec

Right The DB5 shared the DB4GT's cowled headlamps. This 1964 car is seen at the Midland Motor Museum.

The rear lights were changed again for the Series 4 later in 1961, along with a revised radiator grille and smaller bonnet scoop. An oil cooler was standard, though not all cars appear to have had one fitted, and a very attractive convertible version was introduced. The final Series 5 DB4 introduced in 1962 was the most obviously different, as it was slightly longer and had a higher roof to improve interior space. Most of these Series 5 cars were supplied in Vantage form with the DB4GT nose, and in this form there is very little to differentiate it from the car that was to succeed it, the DB5. So little in fact that the most famous DB5 of all – the car that starred in the James Bond film *Goldfinger* in 1965 – was a prototype which had begun life as a Series 5 DB4 Vantage…

Right The classic interior of the DB5 convertible seen opposite.

There may have been little to differentiate the late DB4 and the new DB5 from the outside, but under the skin the DB5 incorporated dozens of detail improvements, most significantly under the bonnet. Here the DB4's 3.7-litre engine made way for a 4.0-litre unit using a 96mm bore, which had already been employed in the DP215 racer and had been available in the slow-selling Lagonda Rapide since 1961. Unlike the Lagonda, the DB5 had three SU carburettors and a claimed power output of 282bhp, giving it a similar top speed to the standard DB4 and acceleration rivalling the DB4 Vantage. At first the DB4 gearbox was retained, with overdrive or a ZF 5-speed gearbox as options; from 1964 the ZF was standard and Borg Warner automatic transmission was offered. Other improvements included a standard oil cooler, an alternator instead of a dynamo, electric windows, Triplex Sundym tinted glass all round, twin brake master cylinders and twin servos. Girling brakes replaced the DB4's Dunlops. Even the jack in the toolkit was upgraded, DB5 owners being treated to a hydraulic item.

As had been the case with the later DB4s, a drophead coupé was listed as an alternative to the saloon, 123 being built. A metal hard-top, with huge wrap-around rear screen, was offered as an optional extra. In September 1964 a DB5 Vantage with three Weber carburettors and a claimed 314bhp was introduced, although comparatively few were made – just 65 out of a total DB5 production of just over 1000 cars. Production of the model ended late in 1965, by which time anyone who wasn't talking about the DB5's spectacular appearance in *Goldfinger* was talking about the DB6 that was just around the corner – and about the new engine that Tadek Marek was working on. That engine was already running, and had been squeezed into the engine bay of a DB4 for testing: exciting times were to come.

Below A 1964 DB5 convertible. The DB5 was the first Aston to carry model identification badges – seen on the bootlid and front wings.

Grand
Touring

With the announcement of the DB4 in 1958, Aston Martin had moved up a gear. For years they had produced fast and well-made sporting cars, which had been rightly acclaimed. But now the DB4 and DB5 had propelled Aston Martin into the top bracket of supercar manufacturers, making cars that were as fast and as sure-footed as anything available anywhere in the world – and at any price.

There were few makers of truly high performance cars of quality. Italy had Ferrari and Maserati, both marques whose reputations had been built on the race track. Lamborghini, with its sights set firmly on producing road cars rather than racing machinery, was only just emerging. France had the individual and beautifully made Facel Vega, packing a 300bhp Chrysler punch and attracting such customers as the redoubtable Stirling Moss. From Germany there were the Mercedes SL sports cars, BMW having temporarily vacated the top end of the market, and Porsche needing until the 1970s to develop the 911 series into a true supercar. Jaguar flew the British flag but their offerings were seen as just a little vulgar, if undeniably effective and astonishingly fine value for money. Britain, though, had Aston Martin.

Buoyed up by the world-wide publicity gained from the *Goldfinger* film, Aston Martin went to the 1965 Motor Show with two new models, the more significant of them being the DB6 saloon. In the same way that the DB5 of 1963 had hidden scores of improvements inside a body which was almost indistinguishable from its predecessor, so the DB6's shape shared much with the previous models, but under the skin the car had been significantly revised. Much of the work on the new car had been completed at Newport Pagnell, where the engineering departments had been moved from Feltham early in 1964. That meant plenty of new recruits; of the Feltham design team only Tadek Marek and Harold Beach decided to follow Aston Martin into the Buckinghamshire countryside.

Previous page 1970 DB6 Mk2.

Below The DB6 looked bigger and heavier than the DB5 thanks to its higher roof and longer rear window, but there was little in it.

Left The cut-off tail and rear spoiler of the DB6 were derived from the 'Project' racers.

Below The first Volante was based on the DB5 platform, and later became known as the 'short chassis' model.

Though clearly derived from the DB5, the DB6 also bore influences of other recent Aston projects. The squarish side windows bore a strong resemblance to the DB4GT Zagato of five years earlier; at the back the vertical tail and its rear spoiler were clearly descended from the wind-tunnel work that had shaped the 'Project' cars. On a 'fastback' body the air flow follows the body shape down towards the tail, but then separates from the car untidily. Cutting the tail short and adding a lip at the top defines the separation

Above Tadek Marek, whose 4.0-litre 'six' reached its ultimate road car development in the DB6.

point, reducing drag and lift, and helps to keep the centre of pressure towards the back of the car to improve cross-wind stability. The DB6's shape, which generated less drag than the DB5's and was more stable at speed, made it a much more effective high-speed cruiser. Once again, racing was improving the breed.

Raising the roof

Though the DB6 looked much longer and heavier than the DB5, in practice it wasn't: the wheelbase was longer, but by less than four inches (102mm), and the overall length increased by just two inches (51mm). Kerb weight rose by just 17lb (under 8kg). The reason it *looked* so much bigger was that the roof had been raised and reprofiled so that it dropped away less rapidly towards the back of the car, in a successful attempt to improve head room. The rear seats of the DB6 were noticeably roomier – in addition to the raised roof, the seat cushions had been slimmed down to save space and the longer wheelbase added legroom. When *Motor* tested the car in January 1966, it noted that the DB6's rear seats could accommodate two average-sized adults, where the DB5 had been fit only for 'two children in discomfort or a transverse adult'.

Less easy to see was that the DB6's body was constructed in a different way to the DB4 and DB5. Again the Harold Beach steel platform chassis was used (still made at the David Brown Farsley factory near Huddersfield in Yorkshire) but the body itself was no longer built up using the Touring *Superleggera* system – even though DB6s would continue to sport '*Superleggera*' badges on their bonnets until Touring's demise in 1967. The DB6's aluminium alloy panelling was laid over a framework of folded steel box-sections, replacing the *Superleggera* system's small-diameter steel tubes. The tubes had been of similar sizes throughout the body structure; by contrast, each box section in the DB6 body could be tailor-made to fit its location and purpose, giving an increase in stiffness and at the same time saving some weight. It was a system which would go on to serve Aston Martin well for many years.

Right Touring's Superleggera badges were fitted to DB4, DB5 and DB6 models – but the DB6 didn't really deserve them.

Radford's 'Shooting Brakes'

London coachbuilder Harold Radford made its name producing 'Countryman' conversions of the more exclusive British marques: if you wanted your Bentley's rear seats to fold down for extra luggage space, you went to Radford. Similarly, the company could oblige if what you really needed was a fold-out platform in the boot of your Jaguar MkIX which allowed you to see over the heads of the *hoi polloi* at Glorious Goodwood or the Henley Regatta. Other options included limousine divisions and fitted picnic sets. Later in the 1960s Radford was famed for its Mini conversions: they made a hatchback Mini for Peter Sellers, and countless specially-trimmed Coopers for The Beatles. In 1964 Radford turned its attention to Aston Martin, but instead of trying to produce a hatchback or folding seats, they went the whole hog – and turned the DB5 into an estate car.

Well, they called it a 'shooting brake' but it's doubtful if anyone ever shot anything from one. The conversion was surprisingly successful, with a long flat roof and very long, rectangular side windows enclosing a reasonable luggage area. The tail retained the DB5's subtle fins, and in side view at least was pleasingly proportioned. A dozen of these cars were made, each one of them starting off as a fully-built DB5.

DB6 shooting brakes were also built by Radford, the bespoilered tail fitting into the estate shape rather better than might be expected – better indeed than the DB5, which had an over-large rear window in estate form. Just seven shooting brakes were made during the DB6's four-year production run, the first of them for Sir David Brown – a car he would keep for many years. Another DB6 was converted into estate form by FLM Panelcraft, who would also go on to build a DBS shooting brake – a rather less happy conversion, its flat roof looking uncomfortable above the curvy side profile of the car's original wings.

The concept of a high-performance estate car was unheard of at the time, but would reappear in later years. Touring tried it with their last-gasp 400GT Flying Star II for Lamborghini, then Reliant put the concept into production in 1968 with the Scimitar GTE. Further Aston Martin estates would follow, but not for some years.

Above FLM's DB6 estate lacked the elegance of the Harold Radford conversions.

Left Radford's DB5 Shooting Brake.

Below DBS Shooting Brake by FLM Panelcraft was the last Aston estate until the 1990s.

1965 DB6 Vantage

Engine:	In-line 6-cylinder, twin-overhead-cam
Bore/stroke:	96mm x 92mm
Capacity:	3995cc
Power:	325bhp @ 5750rpm
Fuel system:	Triple Weber carburettors
Gearbox:	5-speed ZF manual
Chassis:	Steel platform
Body:	Steel box-section body frame with aluminium alloy panels
Suspension:	Front: wishbones with coil springs and anti-roll bar. Rear: coil-sprung live axle located by twin trailing arms and Watt linkage
Brakes:	Girling discs all round, servo assisted
Top speed:	150mph (241km/h)
Acceleration:	0-60mph (97km/h) in 6.3sec

Power for the new car came from a familiar source, the 4.0-litre version of Tadek Marek's alloy straight-six, as used in the DB5. The same 282bhp output was quoted for the standard, triple-SU engine, while the Vantage-spec unit with three Webers was now claimed to deliver 325bhp. Both figures were optimistic, probably by 15 per cent or so. Mind you, Aston Martin's figures were much closer to the truth than those of many competitors: during the 'horsepower race' of the 1960s American manufacturers (or their advertising agencies) were claiming their engines to be 30 per cent more powerful than they actually were, and malleable test 'standards' allowed plenty of room for exaggeration. Anyone competing in that market could either get left behind, or could join in the optimism. Or, as Aston Martin and Rolls-Royce later did, they could keep their horsepower figures to themselves.

The DB5's ZF 5-speed gearbox was also carried forward to the new car, though the DB6 was fitted with a slightly higher-geared final drive giving it marginally taller overall gearing to take advantage of its lower-drag body shape. A Borg Warner Model 8 automatic was a no-cost option, though journalists who drove cars with it fitted were not impressed: in the UK *CAR* complained of the transmission's low gearing, while in America *Car and Driver* opined that no car fitted with that gearbox had ever been 'worth a damn'. But another feature received widespread praise: though the coil-sprung live rear axle located by twin, parallel trailing arms was retained, it now had the DB5's option of Amstrong 'Selectaride' adjustable rear dampers as standard kit. The Selectarides were hydraulic dampers with electrically-adjustable valving controlled remotely by a knob on the dashboard. 'New standards of safety, comfort and stability are yours at the touch of a switch,' Armstrong claimed. That might have been a bit strong, but certainly the Selectaride dampers allowed some welcome fine-tuning of the suspension to cope with a full load of passengers and luggage. The DB6's more comprehensive standard equipment left only two extra-cost options on the list: power steering and Normalair air conditioning.

Right DB6 saloon and, as seen here, Volante models had split bumpers and a prominent oil cooler intake below the registration plate.

Opposite The first of the two Touring DBSC prototypes, based on the DB6.

Volante variations

The second new car announced in 1965 was the Volante, the first of three drophead models of that name to be produced during the DB6's production life. This Volante was based on the slightly shorter DB5 chassis, and as a result later became known as the 'short chassis' model. It had the revised oil cooler duct (under the main radiator grille) and weight-saving split bumpers of the DB6, plus DB6-style rear light clusters. Just 37 were built, two of them with Vantage engines.

A year later the 'short chassis' model was superseded by a DB6-based Volante, complete with bespoilered vertical tail. Alongside it on Aston Martin's stand at the 1966 London Motor Show there was another debutant for the press photographers to aim their twin-lens Rollei cameras at: an eye-catching two-seater called the DBS that had already caused a sensation at the Paris Salon a couple of weeks earlier.

Touring had built two prototypes, a Black Cherry left-hand-drive car and a Dubonnet Rosso right-hand driver, based on shortened DB6 platforms. DB6 front suspension was used, but there was a de Dion rear end with in-board disc brakes. The familiar 4.0-litre engine, in Vantage tune, was mounted 10.5in (267mm) further back than in the DB6 to improve weight distribution. Clothing the whole thing was a spectacular body, nearly 7in (170mm) shorter than a DB6 and said to be 400lb (181kg) lighter. There were echoes of Touring's Lamborghinis and Pininfarina's Ferrari 275GTB in the shape, which somehow still managed to incorporate the classic Aston Martin grille, this time moved below the bumper line to leave a smooth nose. The left-hand-drive car appeared at the show on Minilite alloy wheels, though both cars – later redesignated 'DBSC' to avoid confusion

1965 Touring DBSC	
Engine:	In-line 6-cylinder, twin-overhead-cam
Bore/stroke:	96mm x 92mm
Capacity:	3995cc
Power:	325bhp @ 5750rpm
Fuel system:	Triple Weber carburettors
Gearbox:	5-speed ZF manual
Chassis:	Steel platform
Body:	Tubular steel body frame with aluminium alloy panels
Suspension:	Front: wishbones with coil springs and anti-roll bar. Rear: de Dion with coil springs and Watt linkage
Brakes:	Girling discs all round, servo assisted, inboard at rear
Top speed:	165mph est (266km/h)
Acceleration:	0-60mph (97km/h) in 5.5sec (estimated)

Above William Towns, who styled the DBS, V8 and Lagonda, with his 1990 design for Reliant's Scimitar sports car.

with later Aston Martin models – went on to be fitted with wire wheels. With less weight than a DB6 and a sleeker shape, the DBSC was expected to have a top speed in excess of 160mph (257km/h).

But, promising as it was, the DBSC would not go into production, because Aston Martin had more important things to worry about. Harold Wilson's government was struggling to keep the economy on an even keel, and in the summer of 1966 purchase tax on new cars had been increased, while tax concessions on hire purchase had been reduced. Aston Martins were suddenly more expensive, and the unsound economic climate was making DB6 ownership less attractive. Sales were slow; at Newport Pagnell, production was running ahead of orders and a stockpile of cars was building up. Aston Martin needed new models to encourage new orders, and it needed them quickly. That ruled out any further development of the DBSC – good though it was, it needed too much work before it could be put into production. The engine location, for instance, was so far back in the chassis that it was practically impossible to lift the cylinder head without first removing the engine from the car. The inboard rear brakes were difficult to keep cool. And although the body shape was lovely to look at, it generated front-end lift at high speed. Instead of continuing with the DBSC, development efforts were concentrated on two bigger cars to be powered by a new engine.

Discussions had begun on how to replace the DB4 engine as early as 1962, just four years after it had entered production. Despite the abortive Lagonda V12 of the 1950s – which was developed with half an eye to future road car production – David Brown was still keen to push Aston Martin into an even higher performance bracket, and that meant more power. Greater displacement was the simplest route to a higher power output, which is why Tadek Marek's in-line six had already been expanded to 3995cc. That was its practical limit, although an experimental 4162cc version had also been built. A new engine was needed, and to get a bigger capacity into compact overall dimensions it was decided early on that the new unit should be a V8.

New designs

Plans were laid down for a V8 Lagonda using a stretched Aston Martin platform chassis – a replacement for the ill-fated Lagonda Rapide. But William Towns had other ideas. Harold Beach had hired Towns from Rover as a trim designer; once Towns heard of the plans for the new Lagonda, he proposed a different approach – design a four-door Lagonda, and then shorten it to make a new Aston Martin. Towns' proposal was accepted, though the more important of the two cars to finish first was the shorter, two-door Aston. David Brown wanted that completed for the London Motor Show in October 1967, less than a year away.

While Towns began work on a full-size clay model of the new body shape, Harold Beach set about revising the chassis of the DB6 to underpin a bigger, V8-powered car. The platform was widened by 4.5in (114mm), and the front wheels were pushed forward by 1in (25mm) so that the engine could be mounted behind the front cross-member, keeping the bonnet line low. The double-wishbone DB6 front suspension layout was retained, but at the back there was a new de Dion suspension. It was Beach's favourite system: he had proposed de Dion suspension for the DB4, but it had been rejected at the prototype stage, and a de Dion had been fitted on the Lagonda Rapide. In the Lagonda, the system had suffered rapid wear of the driveshaft splines with noise and vibration as the result. New roller-spline driveshaft joints were now available to make that problem a thing of the past. The de Dion's twin advantages were a reduction in unsprung weight – the final drive was now chassis-mounted, rather than being part of a heavy, sprung axle – and an improvement in traction.

The 90-degree V8 on which Marek had been working was designed to retain the six-cylinder engine's 96mm bore so that the pistons from the old engine could be used in an effort to keep costs down. The stroke of the six was also reduced to 83mm, giving the V8 a displacement of 4.8-litres. Marek also kept the basic cylinder head layout of the six, which meant that the V8 had two chain-driven camshafts on each bank of cylinders, but he reduced the included angle between the valves from 80 degrees to 64 degrees to make the heads more compact. The induction system was arranged in the centre of the 'V', with the exhaust manifolds on the outside of the engine; this meant that looking from the front, the right-hand bank had a similar head layout to the old engines, while the head on the left bank was a mirror image. Thanks to extensive use of light alloy – for the cam covers, heads, block/crankcase, sump and intake manifolds – the V8 weighed about the same as the existing in-line six. The first V8 was running in 1965 and by 1966 they were being driven in DB4 and DB5 test cars.

Both the LB6 and the DB4 engine had been proven in competition before they were released for production, and the V8 had been intended to replace the 4.0-litre six in DP215. But by 1966 the front-engined 'Project' GT cars were obsolete; just as rear-engined cars had replace front-engined cars in Formula One, so mid-engined cars were now taking over in sports car racing. In September 1966 Aston Martin announced a partnership with the racing car constructor Lola, and at the Racing Car Show in January 1967 Lola

Above Lola-Aston at Brands Hatch in 1982.

Below Lola-Aston showing its new 5.0-litre Aston Martin V8 engine.

Below 1970 DBS Vantage, showing its four-headlamp front end.

Above The Vantage engine, with three twin-choke Weber carburettors, was a no-cost option on the DBS.

Right From the rear, the DBS and the later V8 models were almost indistinguishable.

revealed a new 'Mark III' version of its successful mid-engined sports car, the T70. At the same show, the Surtees Racing stand displayed the new Aston Martin V8 engine, said to be producing more than 450bhp in its racing specification, which included dry-sump lubrication and Lucas fuel-injection. Though the T70 had been launched with a Chevrolet V8 engine, an Aston-powered version would soon be under construction. Meanwhile, just a month after the show David Brown slashed the price of the DB6 by £1016 in an effort to clear the stock of unsold cars.

Two Lola-Astons were built, and an assault on Le Mans was planned. Two weeks before the French classic, John Surtees took one car to the Nürburgring for the 1000km race, proving fast in practice but retiring early after the rear suspension failed. At Le Mans Surtees was supposed to share his Lola with David Hobbs, but Hobbs never got behind the wheel: the Lola managed only three laps before a piston failed. The sister car of Chris Irwin and Piet de Klerk struggled on for 25 laps before retiring with fuel system woes. Worse, when the engines were stripped after the race they were both found to be horribly distorted, even though neither engine had been run for all that long. The bottom end of the V8 simply wasn't up to the job. A little over three months remained until the new V8-powered road car had to be on the Aston Martin stand at the London Motor Show; redesigning the engine would take far longer.

So the car that was shown to the press at Blenheim Palace in September 1967, and appeared at the Motor Show the following month, was powered by the 4.0-litre Marek six from the DB6. The standard triple-SU engine delivered a claimed 282bhp, and a 325bhp triple-Weber Vantage engine was available, curiously, as a no-cost option. AE Brico fuel injection was also available. Though the new car could have carried the name DB7, it was instead called the DBS to cash in on some of the good publicity that Touring's two-seater DBS had generated a year earlier. The styling was more modern, with a squared-off version of the now-traditional Aston Martin grille shape, and four headlamps. Towns incorporated a peak at the top of the wings, running the length of the car, which had a hint of the

'gothic arch' wings Frank Feeley had employed on the DB3S. Accommodation was generous thanks to the increased width, and legroom improved despite a fractional decrease in overall length compared to the DB6.

Reaction was mixed. It was well known that the DBS had been designed to accommodate the new V8, and the new engine had failed very publicly at Le Mans just a few months earlier; clearly the six-cylinder DBS with its choice of carry-over DB6 engines was just a stop-gap. Overall weight was up by 250lb (113kg) because the chassis had been designed in a hurry, and there simply hadn't been time to pare away any excess metal. The bigger body also significantly increased frontal area, and with no more power than a DB6, the DBS was inevitably slower than its predecessor, which continued in production alongside it. Aston's managing director Steve Heggie had told reporters in 1964 that the next Aston would do 200mph (322km/h), so the less charitable sections of the press started to question the direction of Aston Martin's development. That said, some magazine road tests of the DBS Vantage still recorded sub-8.0sec 0–60mph (97km/h) times and a top speed in excess of 140mph (225km/h). For a proper four-seater, the DBS certainly didn't hang about.

Redesigning the V8

Back at Newport Pagnell, first Marek and then his successor Dudley Gershon got on with the job of redesigning the V8 engine. The crankcase was stiffened up and the main bearing caps redesigned, and the cylinder head studs were extended down as far as the bottom of the cylinder liners so that their loads were fed into the strongest part of the block. The heads themselves were redesigned to make them stiffer and provide better support for the camshaft bearings. At the same time the bore was increased to 100mm and the stroke to 85mm, to reach a displacement of 5340cc, and Bosch mechanical fuel injection was fitted. At least three DBS development cars were fitted with the V8 engine and road tested for many thousands of miles during 1968 and 1969. By the time they had finished, the V8 was a strong engine, safe to 7000rpm and happy to run all day at its placarded limit of 6000rpm. And it was just 30lb (13.6kg) heavier than the Marek six.

An early V8 was also installed in a new car for David Brown's own use. This was William Towns' four-door Lagonda, the car which had been sidelined in favour of the two-door DBS during the crisis of 1966. It was running by 1969, by which time Aston Martin was receiving a welcome boost from another association with James Bond: the DBS was appearing in *On Her Majesty's Secret Service*, though with nowhere near the starring role that the DB5 had enjoyed in *Goldfinger*.

In August 1969 Aston Martin announced a Mark 2 version of the DB6. AE Brico fuel injection, already available on the DBS, was now a £299 option that would attract 46 customers over the next year. The wheel arches were flared to allow wider DBS wire wheels to be fitted, and the DB6 Mark 2 also used DBS three-eared hub-caps and DBS seats. Power steering was now standard. A Mark 2 Volante, with similar modifications, was introduced at the same time – but the big news for 1969 came a month later.

At the end of September the press was introduced to the new DBS V8, which sported few external clues to the much greater performance that was available. A small air-dam had been added under the front bumper, as the DBS shape had been found to generate

1967 DBS	
Engine:	In-line 6-cylinder, twin-overhead-cam
Bore/stroke:	96mm x 92mm
Capacity:	3995cc
Power:	282bhp @ 5500rpm
Fuel system:	Triple SU carburettors
Gearbox:	5-speed ZF manual
Chassis:	Steel platform
Body:	Steel box-section body frame with aluminium alloy panels
Suspension:	Front: wishbones with coil springs and anti-roll bar. Rear: de Dion with coil springs and Watt linkage
Brakes:	Girling discs all round, servo assisted, inboard at rear
Top speed:	140mph (225km/h)
Acceleration:	0–60mph (97km/h) in 7.5sec

Below The DBS interior offered more luxury and more space than any previous Aston.

1970 DBS V8

Engine:	V8, twin-overhead-cam per bank
Bore/stroke:	100mm x 85mm
Capacity:	5340cc
Power:	345bhp @ 5000rpm
Fuel system:	Bosch mechanical fuel injection
Gearbox:	5-speed ZF manual
Chassis:	Steel platform
Body:	Steel box-section body frame with aluminium alloy panels
Suspension:	Front: wishbones with coil springs and anti-roll bar. Rear: de Dion with coil springs and Watt linkage
Brakes:	Girling discs all round, servo assisted, inboard at rear
Top speed:	160mph (257km/h)
Acceleration:	0-60mph (97km/h) in 6.0sec

Below The DB6 Mark 2, announced in 1969, was the last development of the DB4 line.

front-end lift at very high speeds – speeds the six-cylinder DBS could never reach, but the V8 could. Cast light-alloy wheels were used in place of traditional wire-spoke wheels, as they were lighter and stiffer, and the new wheels were shaped to draw hot air away from the brake discs, which were now internally ventilated. Pirelli tyres were fitted because they were just about the only ones officially rated for the DBS V8's top speed, though they proved to lack the wet grip of the Avons fitted to the DBS. Spring rates were altered very slightly, to accommodate the fractionally heavier engine. As before automatic transmission was offered as an alternative to the ZF 5-speed manual gearbox, but finally the dreadful old Borg Warner Model 8 had gone and in its place Aston Martin offered a Chrysler Torqueflite – a light, efficient, smooth and robust transmission. Power steering was the only other option. The heavily revised engine proudly proclaimed 'Aston Martin Lagonda' twice from each of its cam covers. At £6897 the DBS V8 was £785 more than a DBS, a whopping £2099 more than a DB6.

Unusually, the power output of the new engine was not revealed, Aston Martin deciding that saying nothing at all was better than having to keep up the kind of subterfuge that was rife at the time. But they buckled before the temptation to show how good this new engine was, explaining that the maximum torque was a not inconsiderable 400lb ft at 4500rpm, and that the torque curve remained above 300lb ft from 2000rpm up to 6000rpm. The sharp technical minds at *Motor* magazine quickly realized that the power output could be calculated from those figures, and deployed their slide-rules to reveal during their road test early in 1971 that they equated to at least 345bhp. Whatever the true figure, the DBS V8 was clearly a much faster car than the six-cylinder DBS, *Motor* knocking more than a second off the 0-60mph (97km/h) time and recording a top speed 20mph (32km/h) higher. They also noted that with the standard 3.54:1 final drive ratio the car was undergeared, and suggested that the optional 3.31:1 ratio might allow the top speed to reach as much as 167mph (269km/h).

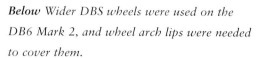

Left The 'Mark 2' modifications also applied to the Volante, as on this 1970 car.

Below Wider DBS wheels were used on the DB6 Mark 2, and wheel arch lips were needed to cover them.

Above Triple SU carburettors indicate that this is a non-Vantage engine.

Left 1970 DB6 Mark 2 Vantage, showing off its bespoiled vertical tail.

For a while Aston Martin produced four models – the DB6 Mark 2, Volante Mark 2 and DBS were now joined by the DBS V8 – but the DB6 and Volante were phased out at the end of 1970, ending a line of Aston Martins that stretched back to the DB4 of 1958, nearly 12 years earlier. By then the DBS had been modified, the lower sections of the nose and tail being reshaped and the air exit louvres in the rear pillars being moved to a panel under the rear window (the prototype DBS had also had louvres in the front wings,

Right To counter front-end lift, the DBS V8 was given a front air-dam. Note the peaked wings, recalling the Frank Feeley 'gothic arch' shape used on the DB3S.

Below The DBS V8's cast light-alloy wheels were designed to draw hot air away from the brakes.

recalling the early DB2s). Demand for the DBS continued to be strong even after the V8 was launched, aided by a widening gap in prices. In 1971 a DBS cost £6210 in Britain, while the V8 was nearly £1800 more than that. But, unfortunately for the company, the DBS wasn't selling in America.

Export endeavours

America had become Aston Martin's biggest export market, and in 1968 the company had opened a new showroom on New York's 72nd Street. But that same year the DBS V8 had been announced, and the American press had carried the story as though the V8 would shortly become available, rather than as advance news of a model for the future. Suddenly nobody wanted a six-cylinder DBS at any price and Rex Woodgate, president of Aston Martin's US arm (and an Aston race mechanic in the 1950s), found himself bereft of customers. The V8, though, was not nearly ready to go on sale in the USA, as it still had to get through the tough American emissions regulations. A great deal of work was needed on the fuel injection system in order to get the car through, which was ironic since the injection system had been fitted expressly because it appeared to offer an easy way of complying with the American clean-air laws. In practice it didn't, and development dragged on far longer than had been intended – that hard-won certification was finally achieved in October 1971, and would only be valid until the end of the year.

It was a difficult time for Aston Martin, with complex and costly development and redevelopment on the one hand and disappearing markets on the other. And it was a difficult time for the David Brown group as a whole. As 1971 neared its end, Sir David – he had been knighted in 1968 for services to industry – finally decided he could carry Aston Martin no longer.

Below Air-exit louvres moved from the rear pillars of the DBS to the panel under the rear window in 1970.

Save Aston Martin

Above William Willson, who took control of Aston Martin in 1972.

Previous page 1973 Aston Martin Vantage.

Below The two-headlamp front end was introduced with the Series 2 V8 in April 1972.

Above Two-tone liveries are rare on post-war Astons – this Series 2 was a one-off.

Sir David Brown had owned Aston Martin and Lagonda for a quarter of a century, and in that time he had seen it create three separate families of cars – each of which had attracted a measure of critical acclaim and customer appreciation. The Atom-based cars of the 1950s had proved themselves on the road and had led to successful sports racers. The all-new DB4 of 1958, and the cars that were developed from it during the following decade, had elevated Aston Martin to the ranks of supercar makers. Now the DBS V8 had shown that the little Newport Pagnell company could produce performance cars every bit as serious as the best of its competitors.

But what Aston Martin had rarely achieved was to make money in its own right. David Brown had not minded: he enjoyed fast cars and racing, and he bought the company as a hobby. In any case, it was good for the rest of the David Brown group if the winner at Le Mans or Monza or Goodwood was seen to be part of the same organization. The money that Aston Martin absorbed could be easily justified as promotional expenditure. That the latest British Ferrari-beater was a 'David Brown Aston Martin' was excellent PR even if, these days, David Brown Gears did have to put up with it being fitted with a ZF gearbox.

By 1971 the picture had changed. The motor industry was more competitive, and for Aston Martin to remain a player it could no longer be treated as a hobby – it had to pay its own way and be managed as a serious business. In addition, the David Brown group as a whole was struggling thanks to the crumbling British economy. Cutbacks had to be made somewhere. With rumours in circulation of seven-figure losses, Aston Martin was an obvious target.

As winter drew in at the end of 1971, Sir David's advisers pressured him to dispose of the company, and as the new year dawned Brown had to admit defeat. In February of 1972 Aston Martin was sold to a Midlands property developer, Company Developments, for just £100 – though the new owners also assumed Aston's considerable debts. David Brown retained a seat on the board. To cover Aston's debts, the company's Newport Pagnell sports ground was sold off.

Company Developments, it was said, had been chosen to take over the company because it was committed to the future of the Aston Martin and Lagonda marques. That certainly appeared to be true when, just three months after Company Developments' chairman William Willson had been installed at Aston Martin Lagonda, two new models were announced. But both of the new cars had, of course, been developed under the previous management.

Two in-house proposals were being considered as the David Brown era drew to a close. The first was a smaller and lighter car, a front-engined V8 with a 'transaxle' – the gearbox was to be in one unit with the final drive and differential. This had been the case with the DBR1 sports car, the main advantage being that the weight of the gearbox was moved to the back of the car, which helped balance the weight distribution. Porsche's 928 and 924, and Alfa Romeo's Alfetta saloons and coupés, would all use a similar system within a few years. The small Aston idea had enormous potential – David Brown said it would have been 'a very fine motor car' – but sadly it never got further than the drawing board. It's interesting to look at how that car might have influenced Aston Martin history. Had it gone into production around 1973-74, it would have made the V8-engined Porsche 928 that was to follow in 1977 look like old news, and it would have stolen customers away from the 308GTB while Ferrari was still trying to figure out whether the body should be made of steel or glassfibre. A smaller Aston might also have put the company in a much stronger sales position during the oil crises and the political and economic upheavals that were to come in the 1970s, and the idea of a smaller and cheaper Aston is one that has reappeared at intervals ever since. But in 1971 Aston Martin was short of money and this was a brand new design that would have needed a lot of time and investment to develop.

Front-end restyle

The other idea being worked on at the time was a revised version of the DBS V8 drawn up by William Towns, who was now a freelance stylist. Towns proposed different styling at the back to improve boot space, and a new two-headlamp front end. The four headlamps used on the DBS had proved to be excellent on main beam but downright lousy when the lights were dipped. With the more conventional two-headlamp layout, the dipped lighting improved at the expense of a slightly less brilliant main beam, but at least the car could now boast adequate lighting in all circumstances. At the same time it allowed a less fussy front end style, with a wire-mesh grille more redolent of the classic Aston DB3S/DB Mark III shape. To solve another problem the new car was also intended to feature good old Weber carburettors, instead of the troublesome fuel injection system.

The front-end styling from that project was what made Company Developments' DBS V8 replacement, released in April 1972, look like a new car. Under the bonnet the Bosch fuel injection was still being used – the carburettor installation was not ready in time – but there were many other useful improvements. A reshaped fuel tank and horizontal spare wheel installation improved the size and shape of the boot, which on the DBS V8 had been short but deep; now it was shallower but longer. Better heat and noise insulation now lined the engine-bay bulkhead, the airboxes changed, and Lucas Opus electronic ignition

1972 V8	
Engine:	V8, twin-overhead-cam per bank
Bore/stroke:	100mm x 85mm
Capacity:	5340cc
Power:	345bhp @ 5000rpm
Fuel system:	Bosch mechanical fuel injection
Gearbox:	5-speed ZF manual (Chrysler Torqueflite 3-speed automatic optional)
Chassis:	Steel platform
Body:	Steel box-section body frame with aluminium alloy panels
Suspension:	Front: wishbones with coil springs and anti-roll bar. Rear: de Dion with coil springs and Watt linkage
Brakes:	Girling discs all round, servo assisted, inboard at rear
Top speed:	160mph (257km/h)
Acceleration:	0-60mph (97km/h) in 6.0sec

Left The DBS V8's fuel injection system proved unreliable, and would not meet the US emissions requirements.

Right The 1972 Aston Martin Vantage was a revised DBS. It was to be the last six-cylinder Aston until the DB7.

Below The well appointed Vantage interior.

1972 Vantage

Engine:	In-line 6-cylinder, twin-overhead-cam
Bore/stroke:	96mm x 92mm
Capacity:	3995cc
Power:	325bhp @ 5500rpm
Fuel system:	Triple Weber carburettors
Gearbox:	5-speed ZF manual
Chassis:	Steel platform
Body:	Steel box-section body frame with aluminium alloy panels
Suspension:	Front: wishbones with coil springs and anti-roll bar. Rear: de Dion with coil springs and Watt linkage
Brakes:	Girling discs all round, servo assisted, inboard at rear
Top speed:	140mph (225km/h)
Acceleration:	0-60mph (97km/h) in 7.5sec

was fitted. Inside, the minor controls were revised and the leather-rimmed steering wheel that had replaced the old-fashioned wood-rim item on later DBS V8s was carried forward to the new car. Obviously the car could no longer be a 'DB', so it was known simply as the 'Aston Martin V8' – although the first few were fitted with 'David Brown Aston Martin' badges. No doubt that was just because they had a few badges left over, and decided to use them up – a time-honoured procedure that had begun with 'Bert' Bertelli and had most recently seen *Superleggera* badges fitted to the DB6.

Alongside the new V8 was a revised DBS, still on rather old-fashioned wire wheels but with the new two-headlamp front end, the triple-Weber DBS Vantage engine and much the same set of improvements as the V8. It carried the name 'Vantage' – confusing given that Vantage models in the past had usually been the fastest and most powerful cars in the Aston Martin range, and yet here it was being applied to the slowest and cheapest model. Some pundits have suggested that Company Developments was trying to get some of the faster models' kudos to rub off on their 'entry level' model. It seems more likely, however, that in the rush to launch the new models they just dropped 'DBS' from both 'DBS V8' and 'DBS Vantage', and ended up with the V8 and the Vantage.

Production ran at about six cars a week, slightly lower than during the last days of David Brown's ownership, but then Aston Martin was now becoming a self-sufficient entity, whereas before it had relied on other parts of the David Brown empire, notably for the manufacture of the steel platform chassis. Most of the cars produced were V8s. Previously production had usually been split reasonably equally between V8s and sixes. Vantages were produced in small batches which ended in July 1973, barely a year after the car had been introduced. At the same time, another revision of the V8 was announced.

Derivatives of the DBS were to be many and various (even by this stage the car was already entering its third major incarnation) and few would be given distinguishing model names. To the undiscerning eye all the cars looked pretty much the same, the odd pair of headlamps notwithstanding. To help bring some order to this chaos, the Aston Martin Owners Club split the cars into different series, Series 1 being the DBS V8 and Series 2 the

Ogle and Other Oddities

The early 1970s saw a minor flurry of Aston-based specials and show cars. Neville Trickett got the ball rolling with the Siva S530, an Aston-powered coupé which won a styling contest run by the *Daily Telegraph Magazine*. The light, mid-engined car, fitted with gullwing doors, attracted plenty of attention at the London Motor Show in 1971, but never progressed beyond the show car stage.

The following year another Aston special appeared, this time as the centrepiece of an all-British display at the 1972 Montreal Motor Show. Styled by British design house Ogle and based on a DBS V8 platform, it was certainly a striking machine, and it was packed with interesting ideas. The body was mostly glassfibre, though above the Ogle-trademark rising waistline there was nothing but a tubular steel frame and tinted glass. The shape of the rear end might just have been the inspiration behind Leyland's wedge-shaped Princess, which would appear a couple of years later, but most people ignored the shape and instead concentrated on the array of no less than 22 tail lights. Four indicator lamps on each side worked one after another, from the centre of the car to the outside, while the row of brake lights below them showed how hard the car was braking – more lights meant a quicker stop. Inside, warning lamps were mounted on top of the dashboard to reflect their message to the driver off the windscreen. A single rear seat carried one passenger transversely.

A running version called the 'Sotheby Special' was built, originally dark blue with gold stripes but later painted white with red stripes and used by Embassy in connection with the Embassy-Hill Grand Prix team. It lived a hard life which apparently ended in a road accident. Ogle built a second running car for Mrs Mary Agate, who coughed up three times the price of a new V8 for the privilege. This one, based on the then-current Series 2 V8, was finished in burgundy with a green roof and had an automatic gearbox in place of the first car's ZF manual. The second car lives on, resprayed bright red and now converted from injection to carburettors. Arguments still rage about the styling whenever 'the Ogle' is mentioned, but its looks certainly aren't improved by the huge bonnet bulge now fitted to clear the carbs!

Above *The Ogle Aston had no less than 22 tail lights. This is the car built for Mary Agate.*
Left *The 'Sotheby Special' Ogle Aston.*
Below *The Ogle interior, in Embassy colours.*

Above Customizing was all the rage in the 1970s, which probably accounts for the Wolfrace accessory wheels on this Vantage.

fuel-injected Aston Martin V8 introduced by Company Developments in 1972. The announcement in August 1973 would begin Series 3.

The new car saw the end of the Aston/Bosch mechanical fuel injection system, which had proved impossible to get through the American emissions regulations and unreliable in service. There were whispers, too, that Aston Martin couldn't afford the rising cost of the injection equipment, and in any case the mechanical injection system was being replaced by Bosch's new 'Jetronic' systems. Using the new system would have meant more development, but instead Aston Martin opted to go with proven technology. In place of the injection system the Series 3 car adopted a quartet of huge downdraft Weber 42DCNF carburettors, the bonnet bulge being enlarged to make space for them. With the carburettors came a start-up technique about which journalists would continue to remark for the next two decades: though a choke was fitted, it was practically redundant. Instead, the procedure was to switch on the ignition so that the electric fuel pumps could fill the carburettor float chambers, fully depress the throttle pedal a couple of times so that the accelerator pumps could richen the mixture in the ports, then turn the key to start.

Back to carburettors

Below For the Series 3 V8, Aston Martin reverted to Weber carburettors. This is the works development car, which was road-tested by Motor *in September 1973.*

The inadequacy of the injection system was underlined by the Series 3 car's driveability with the new carburettor set-up. Though maximum power was probably down a little, low-speed torque had improved, and the Aston would now pull smoothly from very low engine speeds where before it stuttered and surged. As a result of the improved low-speed torque, performance was pretty much equal to the old car, although the example tested by *Autocar* seemed off-song and recorded much slower times. Fuel consumption with carburettors was, if anything, fractionally better than before – though it was still little to boast about, averaging around 14mpg.

Certifying the car for sale in the USA was the next step. Turbocharger specialist Ak Miller developed a turbocharger installation for Aston Martin Lagonda Incorporated, the company's American distributor, which complied with the emissions rules. Back in Britain, Weber said that if the car could meet the regulations with a turbo, then it could meet them without one and work began to prove it. But by the beginning of 1974 Britain was almost at a standstill. The repercussions of the Yom Kippur war in the Middle East were biting, with oil prices rising and western economies once again crumbling. Worse, in Britain a miners' strike led to a three-day working week. Petrol rationing started to look inevitable (coupons were issued in December 1973, though they were never used in anger) and a further blow came in March 1974, when the new Chancellor of the Exchequer Denis Healey announced the addition of Value Added Tax to petrol. Petrol prices soared from 37 new-fangled decimal pence per gallon (8p/lit) in the summer of 1973 to 55p per gallon (12p/lit) by March 1974, and Aston Martin found it increasingly difficult to find customers for their thirsty cars in the home market.

1972 V8 Series 3	
Engine:	V8, twin-overhead-cam per bank
Bore/stroke:	100mm x 85mm
Capacity:	5340cc
Power:	315bhp est @ 5000rpm
Fuel system:	Four Weber 42DCNF carburettors
Gearbox:	5-speed ZF manual (Chrysler Torqueflite 3-speed automatic optional)
Chassis:	Steel platform
Body:	Steel box-section body frame with aluminium alloy panels
Suspension:	Front: wishbones with coil springs and anti-roll bar. Rear: de Dion with coil springs and Watt linkage
Brakes:	Girling discs all round, servo assisted, inboard at rear
Top speed:	160mph (257km/h)
Acceleration:	0-60mph (97km/h) in 6.0sec

Above left The Weber-carburettored V8 had a deeper bonnet bulge to clear the carbs. This was a works demonstrator.

Left The rear view of the V8 changed only in detail from the first DBS to the final V8s more than 20 years later.

Above A quartet of Webers on their manifolds, ready to fit to a V8.

Right Frank Matthews, one of Newport Pagnell's engine builders in the 1970s.

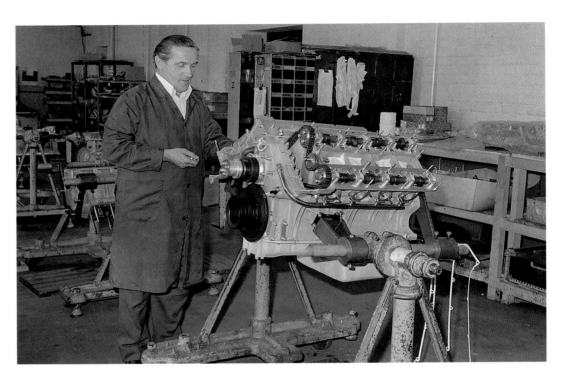

Above The skills of Aston Martin's bodyshop were second to none. Here a panel is shaped on the 'English wheel'.

New models, new management

With work still not finished on the American-spec V8 in early 1974, a decision was taken to delay further efforts until the 1975 emissions rules were announced and to work towards meeting those. Lessons had clearly been learned from the fiasco of 1971, when the car was ready just a few weeks before its annual certification was due to expire. After a five-month durability testing programme which put 50,000 miles (80,000km) on a V8, the US-spec car was finally ready in October 1974. Development though had been costly, and as petrol prices continued to rise, Aston Martin were again facing money problems.

In the midst of all this, at the Earls Court Motor Show in October 1974, the company launched a new model – and relaunched an old marque. Lagonda reappeared, to everyone's surprise, with a production version of the car that had been built for Sir David Brown in 1969. Unlike that prototype, the new production 'Aston Martin Lagonda' had the two-headlamp front end of the latest Aston Martin V8 with a neatly modified grille to give it a family resemblance to the previous Lagonda, the unloved Rapide. At the show, it won a gold medal for its coachwork from the Society of Motor Manufacturers and Traders. The car was 12in (305mm) longer than the Aston, all of which went into the wheelbase to improve legroom, and the longer roofline was also a fraction higher to maintain rear-seat headroom. David Brown's Lagonda had originally worn DBS wire wheels, but had soon adopted the alloys that were fitted to the V8, and the production Lagonda followed suit. William Willson swapped his Aston V8 for the first production Lagonda, which was the show car and which later operated as the company's demonstrator. It was a handsome car with its metallic blue paint and off-white leather upholstery, and was often seen sporting a Union Jack sticker on its windscreen as a patriotic touch.

Launching a new model when the company was so short of money and in the teeth of an economic storm was brave, to say the least. The idea was to attract new business from a slightly different clientele, especially overseas, to open up new markets for Aston Martin Lagonda. Another significant factor was that Willson liked the car, and wanted to see it in production. Despite its styling, which was arguably better-balanced than the shorter V8 that was descended from it, the Lagonda wasn't a success and though it would remain in production for the next two years, just seven cars would be built – each of them costing its owner around £3000 more than the equivalent Aston V8. And the last of them would be made under new management.

Aston Martin was struggling to sell cars in the USA because of its problems getting them through the emissions regulations, and could little afford the costly development work that had been necessary. In the UK sales had slumped because of the Arab/Israeli war and the consequent rapid rise in petrol prices – and public opinion railed against thirsty machines like Astons while there were fuel shortages. Willson approached the British Government for a loan to help Aston Martin complete the work necessary to sell the V8 and the Lagonda in the US, but the Labour government of the time wasn't interested in subsidising the manufacture of luxury cars for the wealthy. With expenses rising and income dropping, William Willson made the decision to extricate himself and Company Developments from Aston Martin Lagonda, and the company was put into voluntary liquidation. On 31 December, 1974, the 500-strong workforce at Newport Pagnell was made redundant, and the factory lay idle. Rolls-Royce, which had weathered its own bankruptcy storm three years earlier, started to take on some of the Aston craftsmen, recognizing the immense skills employed in the Newport Pagnell bodyshop. It looked as though the Aston Martin story was finally over.

The response from the press and the public can only be described as 'astonishing'. Gordon Proctor and Dudley Coram of the Aston Martin Owners Club launched a campaign to raise £250,000 in working capital to get the factory going again. Offers of help flooded in, and one owner sent a cheque for £1000 'to use in any way the company

1974 Lagonda	
Engine:	V8, twin-overhead-cam per bank
Bore/stroke:	100mm x 85mm
Capacity:	5340cc
Power:	315bhp est @ 5000rpm
Fuel system:	Four Weber 42DCNF carburettors
Gearbox:	Chrysler Torqueflite 3-speed automatic (but 5-speed ZF manual fitted to two cars)
Chassis:	Steel platform
Body:	Steel box-section body frame with aluminium alloy panels
Suspension:	Front: wishbones with coil springs and anti-roll bar. Rear: de Dion with coil springs and Watt linkage
Brakes:	Girling discs all round, servo assisted, inboard at rear
Top speed:	146mph (235km/h) est
Acceleration:	0-60mph (97km/h) in 7.5sec (estimated)

Left The Lagonda's Motor Show debut, 1974.

Below Holding the long-awaited US certificate, Harold Beach (left) with Aston MD Charles Warden and Chairman William Willson (right).

Above Four of the seven Lagondas built between 1974 and 1976. Behind them is a 1960s Lagonda Rapide.

Right By the end of 1974 Aston Martin was struggling, and the local newspapers were full of Aston stories.

thought fit'. Cars of all sorts – not just Astons – started to sport 'Save Aston Martin' stickers. In America, Rex Woodgate of Aston Martin Lagonda Incorporated tried to interest people in buying the parent company. One of those people was Peter Sprague, chairman of the National Semi Conductor Corporation, who had read about Aston Martin's problems in the *New York Times*.

Back in Britain the receiver was approached by Alan Curtis, whose business interests included a property company and a flying school. In 1971 Curtis' son Paul had suggested that he buy an Aston, and a DBS V8 became the first of several Newport Pagnell machines

The Aston Martin Owners Club

Few marques can boast an owners club with as long and distinguished a history as Aston Martin, and few one-make clubs can claim such strong ties with their marque.

Mortimer Morris-Goodall, 'Mort' to his friends, began his long association with Aston Martin in the early 1930s, first with an International and then with the 1931 team car, LM7. When A.C. Bertelli found himself unable to build new cars for Le Mans in 1933, Mort ran his own car as a works entry. By the mid-1930s he had formed the idea of a club for like-minded enthusiasts, and S.C.H. 'Sammy' Davis announced in *The Autocar* that an inaugural meeting would take place on 25 May, 1935 at the Grafton Hotel in London. Charles Jarrott became the first President with Sammy Davis as Vice President, and Mort was made Honorary Secretary. Most of the club's activities then were social events, including an annual dinner-dance at the Park Lane Hotel.

Post-war the club was revived first by Dick Stallebrass and then Dudley Coram. Sammy Davis, Gordon Sutherland and Mort Morris-Goodall all took turns as President, and Vice Presidents included such Aston luminaries as 'Bert' Bertelli and John Wyer. In the mid-'70s it would be two AMOC members, Peter Sprague and George Minden, who would save Aston Martin from oblivion.

Today the club's local area groups cover the UK, and overseas they extend from Newport Pagnell as far as Australia and New Zealand. There are many events, both on track and off, the highlight for many people being the annual St John Horsfall meeting at Silverstone. The AMOC celebrated its diamond jubilee in 1995 with a series of events, including a Founders' Day Dinner at the Grafton Hotel. Two years later Lady Paula Brown and John Martin unveiled a memorial to Lionel Martin, which was erected by the club (with support from Aston Martin Lagonda) at the top of Aston Hill.

In 2001 the club moved its headquarters to a restored barn in Drayton St Leonard, near Oxford, which it shares with the Aston Martin Heritage Trust, which had been created in 1998 to look after archives, trophies and the club's Ulster, bequeathed to it by Lewis Treece in 1974. Seven trustees oversee AMHT, three of them nominated by the club.

Healthier than ever, and supported now by a long-term agreement with UBS Financial Services, the Aston Martin Owners Club will be bringing Aston owners and enthusiasts together – and guarding Aston's heritage – for many years to come.

Aston Martin Owners Club
Drayton St Leonard
Wallingford
Oxfordshire OX10 7BG
United Kingdom
Telephone 01865 400400
Fax 01865 400200

www.amoc.org

Above 'Mort' Morris-Goodall, *who started the Aston Martin Owners Club in 1935.*

Left *A high proportion of Aston Martins still survive. Here, 100 pre-war cars line up on the grid at Silverstone in 2001.*

Above Part-built Astons gather dust at Newport Pagnell in January 1975.

Right From the front, George Minden, Alan Curtis, the bearded Peter Sprague and Denis Flather, joined by Aston Martin Sales Director Fred Hartley at the launch of the new Lagonda in 1976.

Above Business as usual at the London Motor Show, 1975. Fred Hartley (left) and Rex Woodgate admire the IBCAM Coachwork Medal.

to be added to a stable already including a Jaguar E-Type and a Ferrari. When Aston Martin went into receivership in 1974, it was Paul who suggested trying to save the company, and Curtis suddenly found his Ferrari and Jaguar sporting 'Save Aston Martin' stickers. He visited the factory, and even demonstrated his faith in the company and its products by ordering one of the unsold cars lying half-built at Newport Pagnell: 'I remember putting a cross in the dust on the bonnet,' he recalled later. By the middle of 1975 Curtis was prepared to make an offer for Aston Martin, but then found out that an American, a Canadian and an Englishman had formed a consortium which had put in a bid of £1,050,000. The American turned out to be Peter Sprague, and the Canadian was George Minden of Toronto.

Curtis joins the consortium

But if Alan Curtis expected that this flirtation with ownership was to be the end of his involvement with Aston Martin, he was in for surprise. A few weeks later he got a call from Peter Sprague, who explained that their original English partner had now pulled out and that he didn't want to continue without a Brit as part of the consortium. When the two men met in August 1975 they found that their ideas for Aston Martin's future dovetailed neatly, and so Curtis became the third Aston shareholder. Denis Flather – an Aston Martin owner for many years, like Sprague, Minden and Curtis – became the fourth a few weeks later.

The Mid-'70s Massacre

Aston Martin wasn't the only luxury car maker to suffer during the economic turmoil of the early 1970s. Rolls-Royce was bankrupt in 1971, though it was the company's aero-engine division that made most of the losses. Government rescue followed, and by the mid-'70s the now-separate car company had overflowing order books.

Less fortunate was another fine old English name, Jensen. Like Aston Martin, Jensen was hit by the spiralling costs of certifying cars for the American market, plus the oil crisis and the social stigma of being seen in such an 'irresponsible' machine. With their big Chrysler V8s, and Vignale styling which wasn't exactly the last word in wind-cheating, the Jensens returned fuel consumption figures which could make even Aston Martins look good. The smaller, more fuel-efficient Jensen-Healey should have saved them, but at its launch it was underdeveloped and inadequate, and never really recovered. Sadly there would be no political fairy godmother to rescue Jensen, and the West Bromwich company was allowed to slip into receivership in August 1975 and close shortly after that, though a spares operation continued to function. Meanwhile, in a few short years £67million of public money would be poured into the ill-conceived DeLorean sports car project in Northern Ireland, to little profitable end.

Panther and Lotus were also troubled during the '70s, TVR had to be rescued again, and Jaguar suffered at the hands of Leyland Cars management (the whole group being nationalized shortly after to save it from extinction). A.C. just about survived by diversifying into other markets, almost giving up on sports cars entirely. And it wasn't just in Britain that things looked tough for makers of high-performance cars. Maserati and Lamborghini both changed ownership, Porsche struggled to convince the world that it could make good water-cooled cars and Ferrari customers started to tire of their cars' sometimes inadequate fit and finish. It was a cruel decade for some of the highest-profile marques in the motor industry.

Above The ill-fated gullwing DeLorean.

Left The pretty Jensen-Healey never recovered from a difficult start.

While the workforce was rebuilt during the second half of 1975, some of the half-built cars that had been gathering dust at Newport Pagnell were completed. Incredibly, despite all the upheaval of the previous few months, Aston Martin appeared as normal at the London Motor Show in October, with a pair of V8 saloons and a Lagonda. As production got under way in earnest at the beginning of 1976, discussions began on creating a brand new car – a spectacular and innovative machine to show that Aston Martin Lagonda was, literally and figuratively, back in business. While the new car would certainly do that, it would also bring Aston Martin a whole new set of problems.

V8 Diversity

Once again Aston Martin had been rescued, this time by a consortium combining sound business sense with a real enthusiasm for the cars themselves. And almost at once discussions began on a new car, to show just what Aston Martin Lagonda could do. William Towns again proposed designing two cars – a short, two-door Aston and a long, four-door Lagonda – which would share external panels to keep development and production costs low. Initially Towns worked on a three-eighths scale model for the Aston, but late in January 1976 the decision was taken to go for the four-door car. Lagonda was to return once more.

Mike Loasby, who had returned to Aston Martin to head up the engineering team, had his work cut out. While Towns worked 12 hours a day on the body, blending the Aston model and a single profile sketch into a complete Lagonda model in exactly a month,

Previous page Aston Martin's stunning 1980 *Bulldog, with its doors raised.*

Right Inside the 1976 Lagonda show car. The interior would be completely redesigned before production began.

Right The first prototype Lagonda sported a curious square 'gunsight' mascot on the nose.

Left By 1977 the Lagonda interior looked like this. The flat, black panels either side of the steering wheel carry touch-sensitive switches.

Loasby and his team set about creating a chassis to suit the Lagonda. The Harold Beach platform, designed for the DB4 and adapted for every model since, was again the basis, but it had to be considerably lengthened: at 17ft 4in (5283mm) the new car was 14in (356mm) longer than the old Lagonda, itself a foot longer (305mm) than the Aston V8. Aston suspension was retained, which meant that the Lagonda kept the well-located de Dion rear end and inboard rear disc brakes. At the other end, a lot of effort went into reducing the height of the engine/ancillaries package so that it would fit under the Lagonda's impossibly low bonnet.

Above The Canadian Bricklin sports car.

Advanced electronics

Inside, the Lagonda was of course trimmed in the finest quality English leather. But the instruments were far from traditional. Ahead of the driver was a blank, black plastic panel with LED readouts and graphic displays for all the usual information (and a great deal more). Peter Sprague had been keen on electronic instruments because he was chairman of an electronics company; Alan Curtis had also been keen because his biggest interest was flying, and electronics had been used in aicraft instrumentation for some years. But the Lagonda's digital instruments would quickly become a thorn in AML's side.

The rest of the car came together incredibly swiftly, despite a distraction in the shape of the Bricklin, a Canadian sports car which Aston Martin briefly examined in the summer of 1976. Originally the Lagonda's launch had been planned for September, with the car to make its public debut at the Motor Show the following month. As it turned out, the press were introduced to the car at The Bell Inn, Aston Clinton, in early October. Though it wasn't yet a running car, it was visually complete and apparently production-ready, though in reality the Lagonda was a long way from being finished.

Above The tiny headlights either side of the grille were just auxiliaries – the main lamps popped up from panels inset into the bonnet.

Right The Lagonda driven by the press in 1977 was later crash-tested at MIRA. Note the glass panel towards the rear of the roof.

Towns' styling was stunning in its boldness. Gone were the 1960s curves of the Aston Martin shape and in its place were striking, sharp-edged lines. At the front there was a tiny chrome-shelled 'radiator' grille (which actually fed air to the gearbox oil cooler) topped by a curious, square mascot. The grille was flanked by two pairs of tiny headlights, but these were only auxiliaries: the main headlamps, again in pairs, popped up from panels sunk into the enormous bonnet. A single wiper cleaned the huge, steeply-raked windscreen. At the back, a glass panel in the roof above the rear seat meant that the Lagonda felt

Left William Towns' sharp-edged styling was carried to extremes: even the exhaust pipes were rectangular.

surprisingly airy inside, despite a cabin that wasn't quite as spacious as the outside dimensions suggested that it should be.

The main focus of attention inside was, of course, the electronics, which were easily the most advanced ever seen in a production car. This was 1976, remember, when most Britons were still getting to grips with the major technological advance that was the pocket calculator, and the digital watch had yet to become a mainstream item. The LED instrumentation in the Lagonda not only replicated all the functions of the traditional instruments in other cars, it also offered the kind of functions now provided by the trip computer in a modern car – data such as elapsed journey time and distance covered, average speed and instantaneous fuel consumption. So much information was available that a button marked 'Essential Services Only' was provided, which when pressed eliminated all the displays except speed, time and fuel level. Conventional steering column stalks were gone: in the Lagonda flat black switch panels, carrying touch-sensitive controls, flanked the single-spoke steering wheel and controlled everything from the electric windows and seats to the automatic transmission.

Stunning styling

The Lagonda's low silhouette was that of a one-off show car, and yet Aston Martin Lagonda assured everyone that, yes, it was going into production. Suddenly they were besieged with orders: around 200 were taken, each backed by a 10 per cent deposit on a price expected to be £20,000. Promises were made that the cars would be rolling out of Newport Pagnell within months – but the problems inherent in sorting out the car's sophisticated electronics had been woefully underestimated. With so many orders in place for the Lagonda, it had looked for a while as if the Aston Martin V8 could be phased out altogether: it was essentially a 10-year-old car, and the feeling was that it was getting long in the tooth. But, instead, it was decided to apply some development to the car to freshen up its appeal: a good decision because it would be many months before the Lagonda would be ready for production.

Top The incredibly fast V8 Vantage resulted from engine development work that had begun with the Lagonda.

Above The big air-dam and the blanked off grille and bonnet scoop made significant improvements to the car's drag coefficient.

Opposite Aerodynamic testing also resulted in the fitment of a rear spoiler to the V8 Vantage.

While work continued on the Lagonda's electrickery, further development effort was put into the V8 engine, first for the Lagonda and then for the Aston. The engine was mounted a long way back in the Lagonda, which helped weight distribution but more crucially gave the engineers a fighting chance of housing this big V8 under the Lagonda's incredibly low nose. Even so, the airbox arrangement had to be altered to reduce the engine's height, and that was found to compromise the engine's torque output. This fact coupled with the Lagonda's immense weight – around 4410lb (2000kg), or two tons in old money – meant that the big car's performance wasn't up to the usual high standard. Bigger valves were fitted, along with lower-lift camshafts to maintain piston/valve clearance, and this enabled the Lagonda-spec V8 to produce the same maximum power and torque as the Aston Martin, but at lower revs.

Parallel to the Lagonda project, Loasby now decided to utilize the big-valve heads to produce a more powerful version of the Aston-spec V8, to exploit some of the potential that Marek's now-robust V8 still had locked away inside. Originally this was to be offered as a kit which could be fitted to existing cars by the company's service department, and the development engine was fitted in a standard V8. At the Aston Martin Owners Club's annual St John Horsfall meeting at Silverstone in 1976, in Mike Loasby's hands, the car confused many with its standard appearance but devastating speed. Soon the decision was taken to develop the engine not as a performance kit, but as the basis for a new model – the V8 Vantage.

Revisions to the engine were conventional, but more wide-ranging than many people realized. As the search this time was for top-end power rather than low-rev torque, higher-lift cams were fitted – re-using the profile from the old fuel-injected V8 which was itself based on the final Vantage form of the Marek straight-six. Cut-outs were machined into the piston crowns to avoid contact with the enormous 2.1in (53mm) valve heads. Bigger inlet trunking delivered more air to huge Weber 48IDA carburettors, sitting on a bespoke inlet manifold with bigger ports. The heads were skimmed to raise the compression ratio slightly, hotter spark plugs fitted, and a bigger exhaust system installed under the car. Once the engine was run in, the result was around 380bhp, with equally impressive torque – too much for a Chrysler Torqueflite, which ruled out a production version with automatic transmission, though automatic Vantages were later built specially for Denis Flather.

Relatively minor changes were made to the rest of the car. The rear suspension was stiffer and the front fitted with a stiffer anti-roll bar on the prototype, though this didn't make it through to the production cars. Bigger Pirelli CN12 tyres replaced the Avons on the standard car. Wind-tunnel testing of the standard V8 (and Robin Hamilton's racer, which we will come back to in the next chapter) showed that big reductions in drag and lift could be achieved with relatively minor modifications. The most obvious addition was the prominent air dam under the front bumper, which incorporated holes for letting in cooling air. Above it, the main radiator grille and the bonnet scoop were blanked off. Perspex covers were tried over the headlamps, but these never reached production. At the back a spoiler was added to the boot lid. With all these modifications in place the prototype Vantage recorded 10 per cent less drag than standard, and lift at both ends of the car was negligible even at the very high speeds of which the car was now capable.

1977 V8 Vantage

Engine:	V8, twin-overhead-cam per bank
Bore/stroke:	100mm x 85mm
Capacity:	5340cc
Power:	380bhp @ 6000rpm
Fuel system:	Four Weber 48IDA carburettors
Gearbox:	5-speed ZF manual
Chassis:	Steel platform
Body:	Steel box-section body frame with aluminium alloy panels
Suspension:	Front: wishbones with coil springs and anti-roll bar. Rear: de Dion with coil springs and Watt linkage
Brakes:	Girling discs all round, servo assisted, inboard at rear
Top speed:	168mph (270km/h)
Acceleration:	0-60mph (97km/h) in 5.2sec

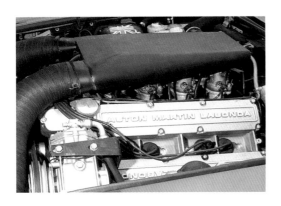

Above The V8 Vantage engine was good for nearly 400bhp.

Above right This red car is believed to be the Marquis of Tavistock's early Lagonda.

1978 Lagonda

Engine:	V8, twin-overhead-cam per bank
Bore/stroke:	100mm x 85mm
Capacity:	5340cc
Power:	280bhp @ 5000rpm
Fuel system:	Four Weber 42DCNF carburettors
Gearbox:	Chrysler Torqueflite 3-speed automatic
Chassis:	Steel platform
Body:	Steel box-section body frame with aluminium alloy panels
Suspension:	Front: wishbones with coil springs and anti-roll bar. Rear: de Dion with coil springs and Watt linkage
Brakes:	Girling discs all round, servo assisted, inboard at rear
Top speed:	143mph (230km/h)
Acceleration:	0-60mph (97km/h) in 8.0sec

Fastest of all

With the standard 3.54:1 final drive it was said that the V8 Vantage had achieved more than 170mph (274km/h) in testing, and with the shorter 3.77:1 axle Aston Martin would claim a 0-60mph (97km/h) time of just 5.3sec, an astonishing time for such a big and heavy machine. It was particularly impressive bearing in mind that the ZF gearbox fitted to the Aston had a 'dog leg' first gear – ideal for fast cruising because it provides a better arrangement for the top four gears, but less effective in a 0-60mph (97km/h) sprint because the change into second (at just under 50mph [80km/h]) isn't so easy. The Vantage, it was claimed, was a fraction faster than Ferrari's 365GTB/4 'Daytona'. And that meant that the new Aston, revealed to the press in February 1977, was the fastest accelerating production car on the planet.

The press, of course, had to find out for themselves. *Autocar* managed a rousing 5.4sec 0-60mph (97km/h) time, even though the car was fitted with the longer final drive, but the car broke before they could attempt a maximum speed run. *Motor* persevered: first the weather intervened, and then, when they got going on their performance tests, they found that the hard-worked press car was off-song anyway. Once the car was restored to health *Motor* took it back to MIRA, where they tried a variety of startline techniques; dropping the clutch at 5000rpm produced too much wheelspin, so they tried 3000rpm, and even that left long black lines of rubber on the road. As they got to know the car better, the times started to tumble – until the Salisbury diff broke. That just goes to show how much abuse a press car has to put up with: nobody *ever* breaks Salisbury axles.

Replete with orders for their new cars, Aston Martin's management now found that they had a fresh problem: the company didn't have the structure within it to manage the production of those cars. A major reorganization was needed. At around the same time Aston's MD, Fred Hartley, resigned. The obvious choice to replace him was one of the four shareholders, but Sprague and Minden were committed to their North American interests, and Denis Flather was retired. Which just left Alan Curtis, so in March 1977 he became Aston Martin Lagonda's new managing director, at the same time trying to restructure his other companies to allow him more time at Newport Pagnell. Four members of Aston's senior management, including Mike Loasby, were made directors. A lot of effort went into getting Aston production back on track, and in particular improving the build quality that had inevitably suffered during the dark days of 1974/75. Curtis later told *Motor* that he bought a magnifying glass, and went round the factory floor looking for faults on the cars. Though he found plenty of faults, he also found a workforce with pride in the cars it made, and with plenty of ideas to improve them. By the end of 1977 Newport Pagnell was building six Astons a week, to a very high standard – and even better, they were selling those cars at a profit.

What they weren't selling were Lagondas. Finding suppliers for the electronics had been a nightmare, and making the whole system work proved to be another. When, finally, the first car was delivered to Lord and Lady Tavistock – old friends of Peter Sprague – not only had it gone up in price by more than 50 per cent but it was also undriveable because the electronics still didn't work properly. A further extensive and expensive redesign was called for, this time using instruments built in Texas and fitted as a complete assembly at Newport Pagnell.

While frantic efforts continued to solve the problems of the Lagonda, another V8 model was also being developed to meet a demand in America. Previous Astons had usually been available as convertibles, but a convertible DBS had never been produced by the factory. Through the traumas of the early 1970s Aston Martin had never had sufficient money to develop an open version, and in any case it seemed that there was little point as new US safety regulations were likely to outlaw full convertibles within a few years. The open cars that were introduced by most manufacturers in the mid-1970s (Jensen, briefly, being a notable exception) featured strong roll-over bars which often compromised their feeling of 'openness' – cars such as Porsche's 911 Targa and Fiat's X1/9. But reports of the convertible's death were exaggerated, and in the end no American legislation appeared to exclude proper open cars from the roads. So the first request Aston Martin Lagonda Inc. made to its parent company, once the latter was back on its feet, was for a convertible version of the V8. The level of demand was brought home to Alan Curtis when Aston Martin visited the Los Angeles show in April 1977 with the prototype Lagonda: very nice, everyone said, but what we really want is an open version of the V8.

Below The drophead V8 Volante was very popular, particularly in America.

Above *Improvements to the interior of the Volante were later applied to the other models.*

Right *Even with the hood raised, the Volante was a very handsome machine.*

1978 V8 Volante	
Engine:	V8, twin-overhead-cam per bank
Bore/stroke:	100mm x 85mm
Capacity:	5340cc
Power:	300bhp @ 6000rpm
Fuel system:	Four Weber 42DCNF carburettors
Gearbox:	5-speed ZF manual or Chrysler Torqueflite automatic
Chassis:	Steel platform
Body:	Steel box-section body frame with aluminium alloy panels
Suspension:	Front: wishbones with coil springs and anti-roll bar. Rear: de Dion with coil springs and Watt linkage
Brakes:	Girling discs all round, servo assisted, inboard at rear
Top speed:	140mph (225km/h)
Acceleration:	0-60mph (97km/h) in 7.5sec

Volante revived

The new convertible revived the name 'Volante', last seen seven years earlier on a drophead version of the DB6 Mark 2. Mechanically it was identical to the V8 saloon, though its front-end looks were smoothed out a little by the adoption of a new bonnet with a bulge instead of a scoop – in effect a neater version of the Vantage's blanked-off look. Inside, the V8's leather was retained, but the interior was restyled and the dashboard was treated to burr walnut facings. The big news, of couse, was the new convertible roof designed by George Mosely, whose track record included designing the Corniche convertible hood for Rolls-Royce. Unlike many other convertible roofs, this one complemented the styling of the rest of the car when it was erected, and when it was folded down it almost disappeared out of sight, despite which it didn't compromise interior space at all – though the already small boot was reduced to a tiny 5.1cu ft (0.14m³). The hood was electrically operated (as it had been on Volantes since 1966) and was wired so that it would only operate with the handbrake engaged and, consequently, while the car was stationary. The new Volante was a wonderfully elegant car, and was very well received on both sides of the Atlantic. However, initially production was entirely destined for the North American market. It was a fitting swansong for Harold Beach, as it was the last model in which he was involved before his retirement from Aston Martin, after nearly 40 years with the company, in 1978.

Shortly after the Volante came a package of revisions to the basic saloon, known at Newport Pagnell as 'Oscar India' – pilot-speak for the letters 'O' and 'I', denoting 'October introduction'. Oscar India (otherwise known as the Series 4) combined some of the body and interior improvements that had appeared with the Vantage and Volante. A smoothed-out version of the Vantage's tail spoiler was now neatly integrated into the rear bodywork, instead of being an add-on extra, the scoopless Volante bonnet was used, and

Aston's MG

By the end of the 1970s plenty of pundits were saying that the Aston Martin V8 was old-fashioned and outmoded, but it was a mere stripling compared to the MG sports cars in production a few miles away at Abingdon – the MGB and Midget, both still selling well, were products of the early 1960s. Instead of developing the cars for the future, the management at MG's owner British Leyland decided instead to cease production, and to close the Abingdon factory.

Within a month of that move being made public, Alan Curtis had offered to buy MG and the Abingdon factory from the state-owned car maker. Curtis saw much the same potential at Abingdon as he had at Newport Pagnell. Here was a car maker with a strong image and a glorious history, with a workforce that believed in the product and that wanted to make the cars.

William Towns produced a facelift for the MGB roadster, and a prototype was built at Newport Pagnell in 1980. The deeper windscreen and door glasses from the hard-top MGB GT were used, and a new folding roof was hurriedly made up using Triumph Spitfire components. A deep air dam was fitted at the front under the universally-disliked 'rubber' bumper. There wasn't time to engineer an alternative to these bumpers, so instead Towns fitted deep black rubbing strips along the sides of the car. This visually lowered the car, and gave it a more harmonious look. A mock-up rear panel incorporated fog and reversing lights, and an inset number plate. Given that the changes were simple and cheap, the revised car looked very attractive.

Towns also designed a replacement for the MGB, a roadster with a detachable boot lid that could be fitted with different hard tops – either a full-length fastback, like the MGB GT, or a notchback coupé. In its latter form the proposed MG looked a lot like the Subaru XT coupé that would appear a few years later.

Sadly nothing came of the proposals, as Alan Curtis could not secure sufficient financial backing to make the project viable, and so Aston Martin Lagonda made just one MG.

Left and below The one-off MGB restyled by William Towns in 1980.

Oscar India had what was essentially a Volante interior with its revised centre console and walnut trim. The air conditioning was also much improved. When the revised car appeared at the Motor Show – held for the first time at the National Exhibition Centre near Birmingham – Aston Martin were delighted to be inundated with orders that would take them right through 1979 and well beyond. By then the Lagonda had been radically rethought, not least in terms of price, and at last the electronics had been sorted out and the car was in production. One of the first of them to be delivered went to William Towns, who had been allowed to jump to queue to get an example of the car he had designed – though within days he had sold it for a fat profit to a dealer in Lancashire!

Above The 1978 'Oscar India' V8 incorporated many detail improvements.

Below right The Bulldog stunned press and public alike in 1980.

1980 Bulldog

Engine:	V8, twin-overhead-cam per bank, twin turbochargers
Bore/stroke:	100mm x 85mm
Capacity:	5340cc
Power:	Approximately 600bhp @ 6200rpm
Fuel system:	Bosch mechanical fuel injection
Gearbox:	5-speed ZF manual transaxle
Chassis:	Tubular steel backbone
Body:	Tubular body frame and aluminium alloy panels
Suspension:	Front: wishbones with coil springs and anti-roll bar. Rear: de Dion with coil springs, trailing arms and Watt linkage
Brakes:	AP Racing discs all round, servo assisted, inboard at rear
Top speed:	Over 200mph (322km/h)
Acceleration:	0-60mph (97km/h) in 4.6sec (estimated)

While customer Lagondas were finally starting to trickle through, Newport Pagnell was turning one of its development Lagondas into a vehicle capable of much greater speed. The Vantage engine, with its tall Weber carburettors in the centre of the 'V', simply wouldn't fit under the Lagonda's low-rise bonnet, so instead a V8 was turbocharged to produce the same power output. Unlike the turbo V8 in the Bulldog (see 'The Bulldog Breed' panel opposite) the turbo Lagonda retained Weber carburettors, and it used slightly smaller Garrett T03 turbos delivering a little less maximum boost. Still, with automatic transmission, the Lagonda could despatch the 0-60mph (97km/h) benchmark in a fraction over six seconds, well over a second ahead of the standard car, and yet it proved very easy to drive thanks to careful matching of the transmission and engine characteristics.

Both the turbo Lagonda and the Bulldog were revealed to the press early in 1980, and there was more news from Aston Martin later in the year with another package of improvements to the V8 which made the cars more fuel-efficient without harming performance. Development of the 'standard' engine since 1978 had by now added barrel-shaped pistons, revised heads with larger Tuftrided valves, and polynomial-profile camshafts which allowed the valve clearances to be tightened up, making the engine quieter and bolstering the mid-range torque output. The compression ratio of the standard and Vantage engines was now commonized at 9.3:1, and both cars now used the freer-flowing Vantage exhaust. Yet more detailed modifications were made over the next few months: interior release switches were added for the boot lid and fuel filler caps, along with central locking, electric mirrors and gas struts for the bonnet. Automatic models now received a new version of the Torqueflite transmission with a lock-up in top gear to improve fuel economy, and came with the option of a cruise control.

During 1980 two new investors appeared at Aston Martin, in the shape of Victor Gauntlett and CH Industrials, a group which included the Coventry Hood and Sidescreen company. By 1981 CH Industrials and Gauntlett's oil business, Pace Petroleum, had

The Bulldog Breed

Since its rebirth in 1975 Aston Martin Lagonda had clearly wanted to show the world that it was a force to be reckoned with, and the razor-edged Lagonda was the first part of that process. The second part, a supercar called Bulldog, had another futuristic William Towns shape and was in some ways an even more stunning achievement.

Work began on the Bulldog as far back as 1976, but it ground to a halt amid the problems with the Lagonda and the departure of engineering director Mike Loasby to DeLorean. Work restarted in 1979, project manager Keith Martin and a small team working in a small area of the factory which inevitably became known as the 'kennel'. The car they built was based around a multi-tube spaceframe, which was originally planned to have de Dion suspension at both ends but ended up with Aston's conventional de Dion rear/wishbone front set-up. The compression ratio of the mid-mounted V8 engine was reduced to 7.5:1 using forged Cosworth pistons, and two Garrett AiResearch T04B turbochargers were fitted. Bosch mechanical fuel injection, dropped from production V8s seven years earlier, made a reappearance as it reduced the height of the engine. Power was said to be 60 per cent more than the Vantage, which meant around 600bhp.

The interior, for two, featured typically high-quality Aston appointments and a development of the Lagonda's electronic instruments, now using liquid crystal displays. The whole lot was clothed in an outrageous 'double wedge' William Towns shape, just 43in (1092mm) tall, with enormous gullwing doors operated electro-hydraulically – the controls were hidden under flaps sited just behind the front wheels. The doors wrapped around and under the car to make entry easier and because of the 'tumblehome' of the sides of the car, it was said that the doors could open far enough to allow egress even if the car had rolled onto its roof.

The Bulldog was completed in under a year and shown to the press in March 1980, with talk of a top speed in excess of 200mph (322km/h). The best achieved was 192mph (309km/h) at MIRA, where tyre scrub on the banking would certainly have limited the Bulldog's maximum. Plans to run the car on Volkswagen's test track, which has a five-mile (8km) straight, came to naught: with a longer final drive it had been hoped that the Bulldog would achieve over 230mph (370km/h).

Only one Bulldog was made. It was sold to the Middle East in 1982, resurfacing a couple of years ago with a light/dark metallic green colour scheme in place of the original champagne and cream, and with garish white leather interior instead of the original, conservative brown. Though never tested to its limit, the Bulldog is still the fastest roadgoing Aston ever built. So far…

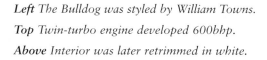

Left *The Bulldog was styled by William Towns.*
Top *Twin-turbo engine developed 600bhp.*
Above *Interior was later retrimmed in white.*

Right The late Victor Gauntlett, Aston Chairman from 1981-91, posing with DBR2/2 which he then owned.

Above A handful of these Tickford Lagondas were sold, at £85,000 a piece. All-white cars were the fad in 1983.

bought a controlling interest in Aston Martin. Faced with another oil crisis and economic recession, the new owners concentrated on improving production efficiency and keeping Aston Martin going. In 1982 the Lagonda was certified for sale in the US, having already earned plenty of customers in the Middle East, and in 1983 both the Lagonda (it had stopped being an Aston Martin Lagonda a couple of years earlier) and the V8 models were fitted with bigger BBS wheels and low-profile tyres. A year later the Lagonda's LED instruments were replaced by tiny computer screens. There was much talk around this time of a 'new DB4', but that never turned into anything concrete beyond some sketches by William Towns (apparently re-using his MG ideas) and speculative magazine articles. Instead it was the existing cars that weathered the storm for Aston Martin Lagonda.

By 1984 the CH Industrials group had departed from Newport Pagnell, to be replaced by Automotive Investments, a company owned by the Greek Papanicolau and Livanos families. When the dust finally settled, Peter Livanos was Aston's majority shareholder, with Victor Gauntlett controlling the balance of the shares. After several years where the focus had been on keeping Aston Martin going through yet another economic bad patch, Gauntlett and Livanos were now keen to expand the company's horizons. At the Geneva show in March 1984, where Italian styling house Zagato had a stand adjacent to Aston Martin's, discussions began that would culminate exactly a year later in the announcement of a new car – the Aston Martin Vantage Zagato.

A new Zagato

Intended to top 300km/h (186mph) and beat five seconds for the 0-60mph (97km/h) dash, the new two-seater was based on the V8 Vantage but had to be shorter, lighter and more powerful. Years before, the DB4's steel platform chassis had its wheelbase shortened for the DB4GT Zagato, but this time the plan was to retain the standard wheelbase and reduce the car's overhangs, particularly at the rear. With lightweight bodywork it was expected that the Zagato would weigh about 3600lb (1633kg), some 10 per cent lighter than the Vantage. While Zagato worked on the body, Aston Martin engineers prepared a V8 Vantage 'mule' to develop the engine and suspension. To reduce the Vantage's weight to that of the Zagato, the air conditioning, seats and trim were also removed, Perspex windows fitted, and the rear valance and spare wheel well were all removed. A revised running gear package was developed using variable-rate springs and dampers, a reduction in castor angle, and new 16in wheels. After extensive testing Goodyear Eagle tyres were chosen as they seemed to suit the chassis better than the Pirellis used on the Vantage.

Above Zagato's trademark 'double bubble' roof shows clearly on this scale model of the Vantage Zagato.

Left Peter Livanos (left), Prince Michael of Kent (centre) and Victor Gauntlett at Le Mans in 1989.

1986 Vantage Zagato	
Engine:	V8, twin-overhead-cam per bank
Bore/stroke:	100mm x 85mm
Capacity:	5340cc
Power:	432bhp @ 6200rpm
Fuel system:	Four Weber 50IDA carburettors
Gearbox:	5-speed ZF manual
Chassis:	Steel platform
Body:	Steel box-section body frame with aluminium alloy panels
Suspension:	Front: wishbones with coil springs and anti-roll bar. Rear: de Dion with coil springs and Watt linkage
Brakes:	Girling discs all round, servo assisted, inboard at rear
Top speed:	186mph (299km/h)
Acceleration:	0-60mph (97km/h) in 4.8sec

Above right The Vantage Zagato rekindled the partnership with the Italian coachbuilder.

Below The use of carburettors on the Zagato engine dictated the addition of a bonnet bulge.

As with the DB4 GT Zagato, Aston Martin were to build chassis which would then be sent to Italy to be bodied and trimmed. Zagato's body turned out to be very similar to the styling sketches and incorporated two traditional features – a version of the Aston Martin grille shape and Zagato's trademark 'double bubble' roof. The initial drag coefficient was a very commendable 0.29, rising to 0.33 after wind-tunnel testing revealed a need for a front air dam and boot-lid spoiler to reduce high-speed lift.

Weber-Marelli fuel injection was now being developed for the standard V8s, and it had been intended that a fuel-injected Vantage V8 would deliver the extra power needed for the Zagato. Sadly the Vantage injection programme stalled, as work concentrated on the more important task of readying the V8 saloon injection system for its launch early in 1986. Instead the extra power was derived from an engine specification originally built for a South African customer, using bigger carburettors and different camshafts. A productionized version for the Zagato generated 432bhp, but it came with a problem: the Zagato bonnet line had been drawn with a low-rise injection engine in mind, and with those big Weber carburettors sticking up out of the 'V' of the engine it wouldn't fit. Newport Pagnell's development car, registered C779DRO and featured in many magazine articles at the time, was given an unsightly bonnet bulge to clear the carbs, while Zagato penned a subtler bulge for the production cars.

Fuel-injection comeback

At the New York show in January 1986 the 'Series 5' V8 was announced, with a fuel-injected engine and an official power figure – 305bhp. Though that figure does not compare well with the outputs seen in the early 1970s, the Aston V8 had suffered more than most because of the gradual tightening of emissions laws on both sides of the Atlantic. With fuel injection fitted – and with ignition and injection controlled by a powerful engine management system – it was a significantly cleaner engine than ever before. And it would now start first time, every time: the big Webers, sitting in the 'V' of the engine, had sometimes suffered from fuel vaporization and a hot V8 had required much churning on the starter before it would fire. The same engine went into the Volante, and both cars could now be fitted with a much flatter and neater bonnet, because of the reduction in height of the engine. The V8 Vantage, meanwhile, retained its quartet of Weber carbs and its bulged 'Oscar India' bonnet.

A couple of months later, at the Geneva show, the public saw the new Vantage Zagato for the first time. A production run of just 50 cars was planned, all of which had been sold months earlier. All that remained was for someone to prove that the Zagato would, indeed do 186mph (300km/h) and 0-60mph (97km/h) in less than 5.0sec. That honour went to the French magazine *Sport Auto*, and although they clocked 'only' 299km/h (185.8mph) that was close enough – and 0-60mph came up in 4.8sec. Press reaction to the car was generally favourable, though there were comments about the styling – particularly the bonnet bulge, which of course was bigger and uglier on the development car that most of the journalists drove – and suggestions that Zagato's build quality wasn't up to Newport Pagnell's very high standards.

Production got under way that summer, and at the same time Aston Martin Lagonda acquiring a 50 per cent stake in Zagato. In October the 432bhp engine was offered as an option on the V8 Vantage and for the first time a Vantage Volante was offered, fitted with rather gauche extended wheel arches and sills. The momentum continued at Geneva early in 1987, where an open-top version of the Zagato was shown and plans were announced for an even shorter production run than the Vantage Zagato, of just 25 cars. The Volante Zagato, as the open car was called, used the fuel-injected engine so that the bonnet could

Above Luca, Elio and Gianni Zagato with the wooden buck for the Vantage Zagato.

Below The Vantage Zagato badge.

Bottom The Vantage Volante of 1986.

Right The skirts and spoilers of the Vantage
Volante were at odds with the 1960s body.

Right The Volante Zagato show car, a modified
saloon. Note the bonnet bulge, which
disappeared from the production cars.

Below The production Volante Zagato.

Left *The revised Lagonda introduced in 1987 featured softer lines.*

Left *Yet another instrument system was fitted to the Lagonda in 1987, this time using vacuum fluorescent displays.*

1988 Volante Zagato

Engine:	V8, twin-overhead-cam per bank
Bore/stroke:	100mm x 85mm
Capacity:	5340cc
Power:	305bhp @ 6200rpm
Fuel system:	Weber-Marelli engine management
Gearbox:	5-speed ZF manual
Chassis:	Steel platform
Body:	Steel box-section body frame with aluminium alloy panels
Suspension:	Front: wishbones with coil springs and anti-roll bar. Rear: de Dion with coil springs and Watt linkage
Brakes:	Girling discs all round, servo assisted, inboard at rear
Top speed:	160mph (257km/h) (estimated)
Acceleration:	0-60mph (97km/h) in 6.5sec (estimated)

be flat as Zagato had originally intended, and it had a revised front end with the flaps over the lights as seen on Zagato's original drawings. That said, some cars were fitted with the Vantage Zagato front end, and some had Vantage Zagato engines, necessitating a bonnet bulge. At the same show a revised Lagonda made its debut: there was a similar but more rounded bodystyle and yet another instrument display system, this time using vacuum fluorescent displays.

The Zagato project had proved that Aston Martin could still make performance cars every bit as fast as the best of the opposition, but they were only ever going to be made in tiny numbers. With the V8 now looking decidedly dated, Newport Pagnell needed to produce a convincing mainstream replacement – a car that could sell in what, for Astons, were large numbers. It had to be a car bristling with modern emissions and safety technology. To get that right Aston Martin needed a motor industry partner with real clout – and that was what it was about to get.

Racing
Returns

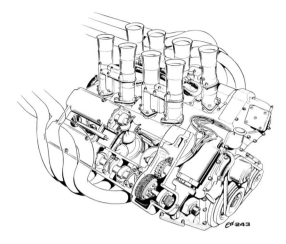

Above The V8 engine which made its debut in the Lola-Astons would go on to power a series of endurance sports cars.

Previous page 1990 Aston Martin AMR1 chassis number AMR2/06.

Below Ray Taft's famous Hyde Vale DBS had plenty of input from Newport Pagnell.

S ince the failure of the Lola-Astons in 1967, Aston Martin had stayed away from international motor racing. But private owners were still racing Astons of all sorts enthusiastically in club events, and by the mid-1970s there was a concerted effort to get Aston Martin racing again at the scene of its greatest triumph – Le Mans.

Midlands Aston specialist Robin Hamilton had campaigned an early DBS V8 in British events from 1974. The car had been practically standard then, but it was gradually modified further and further – sometimes with a little help from the factory, who provided wind-tunnel and engine test-bed time. Hamilton's DBS also gained a two-headlamp front end to keep it looking fresh. By 1976 he was keen to enter the car for the 24-hour race at Le Mans, but a lack of sponsorship meant he had to wait until 1977 to enter the Aston for the Sarthe classic. London company SAS provided some backing, and enthusiastic AMOC members even dipped into their own pockets to help out. John Wyer, Aston Martin's racing manager in the 1950s, was a consultant to the project. By now the Aston was so heavily modified that Hamilton had given it a new chassis number, RHAM1.

Hamilton ran the car at the Silverstone Six Hours in May 1977 as a dry-run for Le Mans, partnered by club racer David Preece (who would be sharing the car with Hamilton and Mike Salmon at Le Mans). Preece spun the car in practice, fortunately without major damage. In the early part of the race the car ran well and looked likely to finish in the top 10. After two hours Hamilton came in for a scheduled stop to hand over to Preece, but while the car was stationary in the pits heat soak from the huge inboard rear brakes cooked one of the final-drive oil seals, causing an oil leak. Nearly an hour was lost making repairs, and the Aston finished the race at such a reduced pace (in an effort to preserve the axle) that it failed to qualify as a finisher. As had happened 10 years earlier with the Lola-Astons, the race had been a failure, but the lessons learned had been invaluable. For Le Mans the rear brake cooling was improved, and an oil circulation system rigged up to keep the differential cool.

Wind-tunnel testing had shown that aerodynamic lift was a problem at the rear of the Aston at the very high speeds it would reach along the Mulsanne straight. The car had been built to run in Group 4, for modified production cars, but with a rear spoiler fitted to reduce lift it now slipped into Group 5, where it was up against turbocharged Porsche 935s and BMW 320s. At Le Mans, Hamilton realized that the Aston was also eligible for the GT Prototype (or 'GTP') class where competition was less fierce, and he made a last-minute deal with the organizers to swap classes. After practice it was touch and go whether the Aston would be allowed to race, as it had qualified slowest in its class and the organizers had decided to drop the last qualifier in each class to reduce the size of the grid. Fortunately another GTP entry was deemed to have infringed the regulations, and the Aston was in.

V8 at Le Mans

Hamilton took the first stint in the race as he knew the car best, and would be most likely to spot any early problems. After just three laps he was back in the pits with a brake vibration, though that turned out to be nothing worse than the pads bedding in. More serious brake problems surfaced just after 10p.m., when the front discs were found to be cracked. Replacement took half an hour, and forced the team to rely on engine braking for the rest of the race to preserve the brakes because they had no further replacements available – the other spare set of discs had been used during practice. Other minor problems included leaks from the differential oil tank and a broken gearlever, which Mike Salmon threw out of the window in case it rolled around on the floor and got caught under the pedals. A French marshal retrieved it and ran all the way to the Hamilton pit to return it. Despite these worries the big Aston raced on, and it crossed the line to finish in 17th place overall and third in the GTP class. It was an excellent result, and one which added to the joy of the large British contingent of spectators who were already celebrating fifth place for the Alain de Cadenet/Chris Craft Lola. Ironically, had the Aston been entered in Group 5 as Hamilton had originally planned, it would have finished second in class.

For 1978 Hamilton planned to return to Le Mans with a turbocharged engine developing around 800bhp but, in testing, the car's fuel consumption was horrendous – sometimes a low as 2.5mpg, more than double its average consumption in the '77 event. Even utilizing the larger fuel tank that was allowed under GTP regulations, it just wasn't practical to run at Le Mans, as the Aston would spend too long in the pits being refuelled. It was withdrawn a couple of weeks before the race. Hamilton added fuel injection, which improved consumption to a more practicable 4.0mpg, and in this form the car reappeared at the Silverstone Six Hours in May 1979 driven by Hamilton and sports car superstar Derek Bell. Brake and oil breather problems dogged the car at Silverstone, and there would be no fairytale ending at Le Mans that year either, as the car holed a piston less than three hours into the race. That was very nearly the end for RHAM1's competition career, but there was one final outing which was very different, and much more successful – an attempt on the speed record for towing a caravan. On the long runway at RAF Elvington it achieved 124.91mph (201.02km/h) over a flying quarter mile.

Rather than develop the turbo Aston further, Robin Hamilton now felt that the best option was to use the reliable and relatively frugal non-turbo V8 in a purpose-built racing

1977 DBS V8 RHAM1	
Engine:	V8, twin-overhead-cam per bank, dry sump lubrication
Bore/stroke:	100mm x 85mm
Capacity:	5340cc
Power:	520bhp @ 6750rpm
Fuel system:	Four Weber 50IDA carburettors
Gearbox:	5-speed ZF manual
Chassis:	Steel platform
Body:	Steel box-section body frame with aluminium alloy panels
Suspension:	Front: wishbones with coil springs and anti-roll bar. Rear: de Dion with coil springs and Watt linkage
Brakes:	Lockheed discs all round, inboard at rear
Top speed:	188mph (303km/h)
Acceleration:	0-60mph (97km/h) in 5.0sec (estimated)

Below Robin Hamilton's V8 at Le Mans in 1979. It retired in the third hour.

Right The Nimrod Group C car, powered by an Aston V8, was wrong-footed by changes in the regulations.

Right Famous racers of past and present take stock of the Nimrod at its Goodwood launch. Left to right: Stirling Moss, Nigel Mansell, Roy Salvadori, James Hunt and Derek Bell.

Above The Nimrod V8s were prepared by Aston Martin Tickford.

chassis. This would be designed for the new 'Group C' sports car category and the proposed American IMSA series which, it was hoped, would adopt broadly similar regulations. Eric Broadley of Lola was called in to draw up the chassis, an alloy monocoque 'tub' with a tubular rear subframe carrying the mid-mounted engine and Hewland transaxle. It was an ambitious and expensive project and, with Hamilton's limited resources, development could only progress slowly until early in 1981, when he found a willing ally in Victor Gauntlett, the new chairman of Aston Martin. When Gauntlett's partner at Newport Pagnell, Peter Livanos, asked Hamilton to build another car for IMSA races, it became clear that the project needed to be put on a proper footing. In September 1981 Nimrod Racing Automobiles was born with Hamilton, Gauntlett and Livanos as its three shareholders. Engines were to be supplied for the cars from a new Aston engineering subsidiary, Aston Martin Tickford.

Above As with all Le Mans cars, the Nimrod was ostensibly a two-seater.

Soon afterwards it became clear that the IMSA regulations would in fact be markedly different to the Group C rules, at which point Livanos' interest in the Nimrod project rapidly waned. Hamilton and Gauntlett continued, with the focus now on Group C, the 1982 sports car series (which was now called the World Endurance Championship) and the Le Mans 24-hour race. But the finalized Group C regulations put the Nimrod at a disadvantage in weight and aerodynamic terms. When the Nimrod had been designed, the proposed regulations had stipulated a minimum weight of 1000kg (2205lb), but in the final regulations this had been reduced by 200kg (441lb). The Nimrod had also been designed with a flat underside, which the original regulations had stipulated to reduce the amount of 'ground effect' downforce produced by the cars. This rule had now been scrapped: the flat-bottomed, 1000kg Nimrod would be up against ground-effect cars weighing just 800kg (1764lb).

Debut of the Nimrod

The first Nimrod was shown to the press at Goodwood in November, where it was demonstrated by Stirling Moss and James Hunt, and two race cars were built up for a race debut at the Silverstone Six Hours in May. The second Nimrod, chassis NRAC2/003, was to be run as a works effort and driven by Tiff Needell, Geoff Lees and Bob Evans. The third car was privately owned by Viscount Downe, President of the Aston Martin Owners Club, and run by Aston specialist Richard Williams on a much more restricted budget. Experienced Aston racer Mike Salmon and engineer/driver Ray Mallock were to share the driving duties. Williams had stripped and rebuilt the Downe car, and its suspension geometry had been tweaked by Mallock. Williams also imposed a rev limit of 6500rpm, compared to the 7000rpm recommended by Tickford and used by the works car. Engine failures had plagued the works team in testing, and would account for the car in the race, but the Downe car soldiered on despite increasing oil consumption. It finished sixth overall, fourth in Group C, to rapturous applause from the British crowd.

In the run-up to Le Mans the works car destroyed yet more engines in testing, and Mallock again refined the suspension of the Downe car, the improvements lopping nearly

1982 Nimrod NRAC2/004

Engine:	V8, twin-overhead-cam per bank
Bore/stroke:	100mm x 85mm
Capacity:	5340cc
Power:	560bhp @ 7000rpm
Fuel system:	Lucas mechanical fuel injection
Gearbox:	Hewland VG 5-speed manual
Chassis/body:	Aluminium alloy tub with tubular rear subframe
Suspension:	Front: inboard by coil springs, rocker arms and wide-based lower wishbones plus anti-roll bar. Rear: four-link with coil springs plus anti-roll bar
Brakes:	Lockheed discs all round
Top speed:	203mph (327km/h)
Acceleration:	0-60mph 997km/h) in 4.5sec (estimated)

Right *James Hunt and Stirling Moss with the Nimrod next to DBR1/2 (the 1959 Le Mans winner). Jack Fairman is Roy Salvadori's passenger, with Eric Thompson looking on.*

Above *The Nimrod had a suggestion of an Aston Martin shape about its front air intake.*

two seconds off the car's lap time at Silverstone. At Le Mans, where Simon Phillips joined Mallock and Salmon in the Downe car, both teams fell foul of the scrutineers – a regular problem for British teams at Le Mans. The Nimrod windscreens were deemed to be below the regulation minimum height. Hamilton raised the ride height on the works car, solving the problem but compromising the handling, while Williams fitted an extension 'bubble' above the screen of the Downe car, leaving the handling unsullied but reducing top speed along the Mulsanne straight by 7mph (11km/h) because of the additional drag. The 'bubble' looked a bit like the roof light on one of London's black cabs, and come race day it had acquired the legend 'TAXI'.

The works car experienced tyre problems in practice, its higher top speed along Mulsanne causing the rear tyres to 'grow' away from the rims and lose pressure. Three hours into the race the same thing happened again, a tyre failure pitching a helpless Tiff Needell into the barriers. Needell, who walked away from the shunt, later said he'd always wondered what happened if you turned right at 200mph (322km/h), and now he knew. The Downe car, meanwhile, steadily rose through the field as its excellent fuel economy – compared to some of the turbocharged opposition – saved it time in the pits refuelling. While the shaken Needell was making his way back to the pits, the private Nimrod was 10th, and by midnight it was running a creditable sixth. By 4a.m. the leading Rondeau had retired and one of the front-running Porsches was sick, promoting the Nimrod to fourth place – the leading non-turbo car, and leading non-Porsche. But half the race was still to run...

Trouble struck with five and a half hours to go. Failing fuel pressure had caused the mixture to go weak, resulting in a burnt-out exhaust valve, and the car was running on seven cylinders. After half an hour in the pits for attention to the fuel system, it rejoined in eighth place, aiming to make the finish. There was another scare at 2p.m. when the car stopped out on the circuit with a dead engine, but somehow Mallock got it going again and limped back to the pits. As the 24-hour race entered its dying minutes the sick-sounding Nimrod circulated slowly in ninth place, then eighth and then seventh as a Porsche and Ferrari ahead of it hit trouble. Victor Gauntlett and Viscount Downe vowed that they would push the Nimrod themselves if that's what it needed to get it across the

finish line, and as the 4p.m. finish time loomed all ears listened for the V8's distinctive bellow. Seven minutes elapsed before the Nimrod completed its final lap, but there it was, to the joy of the thousands of British fans: seventh place overall behind five Porsches and a Ferrari, and fourth in Group C. It was a tribute to the mechanical sympathy of Ray Mallock and Mike Salmon that the Nimrod had made it at all: after the race it was found that the weak mixture had been slowly destroying the valves, and the engine had compression on only five of its eight cylinders.

Above *Viscount Downe's Nimrod battled on to seventh place overall in the hands of Ray Mallock and Mike Salmon.*

By the time the cars got to Spa in September the works Nimrod had suffered a total of 15 engine failures in racing and testing, and Hamilton was becoming more and more dissatisfied with Tickford's engines. Yet another engine failure would put the car out of the Belgian race, but the Downe machine would record a fighting 11th place, seventh in Group C. It recorded a solid ninth at Brands Hatch a few weeks later. Thanks to the private car's reliability, Nimrod took third place in the World Endurance Championship behind Porsche and the impressive Rondeau equipe. But despite Nimrod's fighting effort on the track, Victor Gaunlett pulled out of the project at the end of 1982, beset by troubles with his oil company Pace Petroleum and the daily fight to keep Aston Martin going. Hamilton carried on alone, racing two cars in American IMSA events with his own engines and beginning to build a new carbon-fibre car called the C3, but the cost was just too high. Nimrod was forced to fold at the end of 1983.

Nimrod evolves

For the 1983 season the Downe car had been substantially revised by Ray Mallock and Richard Williams. A new body gave it twice as much downforce, and it was 10 per cent lighter. At Silverstone it recorded lap times in wet conditions that were quicker than the car had previously been capable of in the dry. The redesigned 'evolution' Nimrod made its race debut at the Silverstone 1000 Kilometres in May, where it shared the grid with a new Aston-engined car called the EMKA. This much lighter machine was a Len Bailey design, bankrolled by Pink Floyd manager Steve O'Rourke, who was to share driving duties with Tiff Needell and saloon car expert Jeff Allam. Both Aston-engined cars ran well, the Nimrod finishing seventh and the EMKA running ninth until a detached rear wing delayed

1985 Emka	
Engine:	V8, twin-overhead-cam per bank
Bore/stroke:	100mm x 85mm
Capacity:	5340cc
Power:	560bhp @ 7000rpm
Fuel system:	Lucas mechanical fuel injection
Gearbox:	Hewland VG transaxle
Chassis/body:	Aluminium alloy tub, engine as stressed member
Suspension:	Front: wishbones with coil springs plus anti-roll bar. Rear: inboard by coil springs, rocker arms and lower wishbones plus anti-roll bar
Brakes:	AP discs all round
Top speed:	218mph (351km/h)
Acceleration:	0-60mph (97km/h) in 4.5sec (estimated)

it and finally a wheel bearing failure stopped it, cruelly, just a lap from the end. At Le Mans, the Nimrod broke a conrod on Sunday morning after losing a lot of oil early in the race, but the EMKA fought against a multitude of troubles to finish in 17th place. The Viscount Downe Nimrod appeared twice more that year, at Spa-Francorchamps where a conrod bolt broke while it was running seventh, and at Brands Hatch where it retired with a rare final-drive breakage.

Two-car team

The Bovis sponsorship that the Downe car had enjoyed during 1983 supported a two-car Nimrod team in 1984, the second car being owned by Peter Livanos. Confusion reigned over the fuel consumption regulations that year, FISA (motor sport's governing body) first reduced the fuel allowance by 15 per cent and then changed its mind and left the required consumption at 1983 levels. The Downe car remained in essentially 1983 trim, while the Livanos Nimrod was given a Tickford turbocharged engine and lighter Kevlar bodywork. Neither car finished at Silverstone, and for Le Mans Williams, never keen on the idea of turbocharging the V8, opted to run normally-aspirated engines in both cars. Mike Salmon would again drive chassis 004, the Downe car, but this time alongside John Sheldon and Richard Attwood. Ray Mallock shared the 005 Livanos car with Drake Olsen.

The Nimrods shook off minor troubles early in the race to be running a fine fifth and 13th as night fell. But it wasn't to last: on the 93rd lap, as Sheldon aimed 004 through the Mulsanne kink at more than 200mph (322km/h), a rear tyre failed. The car smashed into the barriers and disintegrated, throwing debris across the track and bursting into flames. Sheldon walked away from the shunt despite serious injuries; flying wreckage killed a marshal and badly injured another. A few seconds behind, Jonathan Palmer's Porsche came upon the scene with Drake Olsen in the other Nimrod right behind and as Palmer braked to pick his way through the debris, he caught Olsen unawares. Olsen swerved to avoid the slowing Porsche, in the process driving two wheels off the edge of the tarmac, with the

Above Steve O'Rourke's EMKA-Aston finished 17th at Le Mans in 1983.

Right The Nimrod team in the Le Mans pits in 1984. Both cars were eliminated in accidents.

Jaguar: Family Rivalry

Two old adversaries battled once more in the 1983 IMSA series, when Robin Hamilton's Nimrod-Astons found themselves up against the Jaguar XJR-5s of Bob Tullius. The 6.0-litre, V12-engined Jaguars appeared at Le Mans the following year and again in 1985, though without success. Meanwhile Tom Walkinshaw had campaigned a V12 XJS in the European Touring Car Championship both as team boss and driver, winning the driver's title in 1984. For 1985 he commissioned a new Group C car, XJR-6, which proved competitive from the outset and won Jaguar's first modern sports car race at Silverstone in 1986. There were no further wins that year, though good reliability put Derek Warwick in the hunt for the driver's title until the final round.

The XJR-8 that followed dominated the 1987 season, winning the teams' title for Jaguar and the driver's title for Raul Boesel, but Le Mans success eluded Jaguar until 1988 – the victorious XJR-9 being driven by Jan Lammers, Johnny Dumfries and Andy Wallace. Martin Brundle won the driver's championship for Jaguar that same year. By the time Aston's AMR1 hit the tracks in 1989, Jaguar was using a new 750bhp turbo V6 engine in its XJR-10/XJR-11 cars. But good results were hard to come by, and when Jaguar achieved its 1-2 at Le Mans in 1990 it was with the XJR-12, a new V12-powered car. By then both marques were part of the Ford empire and the Aston Group C team had been disbanded.

Jaguar won its third title in 1991 with the very fast XJR-14, powered by an endurance version of Cosworth's HB Grand Prix engine. Rule changes then saw the Jaguars leave the international scene – though they would be back with a GT-class XJ220 in 1993.

Below Bob Tullius began Jaguar's sports car revival, with cars such as the XJR-5.

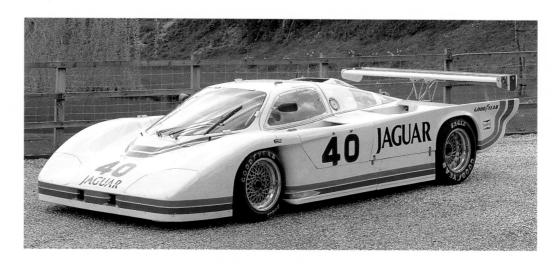

Above The production-based Jaguar V12 engine, seen here in the 1986 XJR-6.

Left The 1988 Le Mans winners, with their victorious XJR-9. From left: Andy Wallace, Jan Lammers and Johnny Dumfries.

1984 Cheetah G604

Engine:	V8, twin-overhead-cam per bank
Bore/stroke:	100mm x 85mm
Capacity:	5340cc
Power:	580bhp @ 7000rpm
Fuel system:	Lucas mechanical fuel injection
Gearbox:	Hewland VG transaxle
Chassis/body:	Carbon-fibre composite monocoque, engine as stressed member
Suspension:	Front: wishbones with coil springs and anti-roll bar. Rear: wishbones with rocker-actuated coil springs
Brakes:	Lockheed discs all round
Top speed:	203mph (327km/h)
Acceleration:	0-60mph (97km/h) in 4.5sec (estimated)

result that the Livanos-owned Nimrod spun into the barriers on the left-hand side of the track, fortunately without injury to Olsen. Cruel luck had eliminated both Nimrods from the race within seconds of each other. They never competed again, Williams and his team instead running a DFV-engined Ecosse car in 1985, in the Group C2 championship – which it won!

But Aston-engined cars continued to appear in the World Endurance Championship. Chuck Graemiger's Cheetah debuted in 1984, using the more compact version of the Aston V8 that Tickford had built for the EMKA. Much lighter than the Nimrod, at around 1918lb (870kg), the Cheetah still struggled to be competitive as its tiny budget never allowed it enough development time to sort the suspension and aerodynamics properly. It continued into 1985, Steve O'Rourke's EMKA reappearing that year in much modified form. The EMKA distinguished itself by briefly leading at Le Mans, where it would finish 11th, though O'Rourke found Le Mans so exhausting that 1985 would be the EMKA's final season.

Victor Gauntlett was not about to let Aston Martin's racing history end there. In August 1987 it was announced that Aston Martin and Ecurie Ecosse were to join forces to build an Aston Martin Group C1 car, to be designed by Max Boxstrom and developed by Ray Mallock. The American company Callaway, then nearing completion of a 32-valve version of the V8 for a new generation of Aston road cars, would be developing a 700bhp, 6.0-litre racing version. Richard Williams would run the team. Initially the car, labelled AMR1, would be developed to assess its potential with no clear commitment to racing it. To hit the tracks, it had to be good, not least because competition in Group C was now far fiercer than it had been a few years earlier. The early 1980s had seen processions of Porsches winning endurance races all over the world, but over the next few years Porsche were being challenged at the very highest level by teams such as Jaguar, Sauber-Mercedes, Nissan, Toyota and Mazda.

Right AMR1's debut, at Dijon in May 1989. It finished 17th, the first British car home.

Below The EMKA's final Le Mans, in 1985.

Developing AMR1

By September 1987, just as Ford was taking control of Aston Martin, the first quarter-scale model of AMR1 was completed for use in aerodynamic testing at Southampton University, where the team could use a moving-floor wind tunnel – essential for correctly modelling the car's complex aerodynamics. Boxstrom's concept was unusual: a Formula One-style carbon/Kevlar tub made up from just three main panels, with full-width ground-effect venturis at the front and rear. The tub's shape and the huge air exit ducts behind the front wheels gave AMR1 a purposeful wasp-waisted stance. To keep the main masses low while still allowing space for the ground-effect tunnel at the back, the Callaway engine was angled forwards in the car and the final drive was offset to the left, with unequal length driveshafts. Wishbone suspension was used at both ends, the rear suspension picking up on the engine/transaxle, the latter a bespoke Aston Martin unit. As on production Astons, Goodyear tyres were now used in place of the Avons of old.

First tests were planned for June 1988, but slipped back to November, where the car used a 5.3-litre, 530bhp engine for its first run in the hands of Ray Mallock, David Leslie and the very experienced sports car racer Brian Redman. Testing continued in January at Donington Park, where David Leslie was unfortunate enough to have a rear hub fail. The tub was damaged in the ensuing accident and, rather than rebuild it, the team turned its attention to the second chassis, AMR1/02, which was already nearing completion and which was slightly lighter. Later that month came the official announcement that Aston Martin would contest the 1989 World Sports Prototype Championship (FISA had been renamed the series again) with cars developed by a new subsidiary company, Aston Martin Racing Development, and run by another, Proteus Technology. Aston's new owners, Ford, had made it clear that the company would not fund the racing programme, so it was Peter Livanos who picked up the bill.

The cars were not ready in time for the first round of the championship at Suzuka in Japan, which meant an automatic FISA fine of £250,000, making a dent in the team's budget of £26million. Two engine failures in testing early in May robbed the team of testing time and were an unexpected setback, the Callaway engines (now in 6.0-litre form) normally revving reliably to 8500rpm. At Dijon for the second round of the championship AMR1/02 struggled with handling problems, made more complicated by the car's high downforce, but its excellent braking was particularly impressive. The Aston finished the French race in 17th place, the team being unwilling to push too hard in such an untested car. It was the first British car home after both of Tom Walkinshaw's Jaguars retired.

AMR1/02 and AMR1/03 were the team's two entries at Le Mans three weeks later, by which time Max Boxstrom had left to concentrate on running his Dymag wheel company. Redman was back in his Dijon car and joined by Michael Roe and Costas Los, while Leslie shared AMR1/03 with Ray Mallock and David Sears. Both cars wore a 'black arm band' across one front wing as a mark of respect for John Wyer, who had died in April. The AMR1s now featured revised noses, and sported a special Le Mans aerodynamic package which included a smaller rear wing which was mounted higher and further back.

Handling woes and a lack of top-end speed due to excessive drag meant the Astons didn't shine in practice. Both cars picked up places in the early part of the race despite instrumentation problems for David Leslie, and a minor 'off' for David Sears. It was all

1989 AMR1	
Engine:	V8, twin-overhead-cam per bank, four valves per cylinder
Bore/stroke:	Not revealed
Capacity:	6000cc
Power:	700bhp @ 8000rpm approx
Fuel system:	Zytek electronic engine management
Gearbox:	Aston Martin transaxle
Chassis/body:	Carbon/Kevlar monocoque tub
Suspension:	Front: wishbones with coil springs and anti-roll bar. Rear: wishbones with coil springs and anti-roll bar
Brakes:	AP ventilated discs all round
Top speed:	217mph (349km/h)
Acceleration:	0-60mph (97km/h) in 4.0sec (estimated)

Below AMR1/02, with its 'black arm band' worn in memory of John Wyer, finished 11th at Le Mans in 1989.

Above AMR1/04 *recorded the best finish of the year at Brands Hatch, a fighting fourth for David Leslie and Brian Redman.*

Below The distinctive 'wasp-waisted' shape of the AMR1 was a result of its innovative aerodynamic design.

going pretty well until AMR1/03's engine failed early on Sunday morning. As other cars retired, the remaining Aston worked its way up to 14th before a suspension joint failed on the Mulsanne straight – though fortunately without causing any damage, Redman bringing the car in for attention. AMR1/02 finished 11th, as the EMKA had done on the last Aston outing at Le Mans in 1985, a lap ahead of the Terada/Duez/Weidler Mazda.

Promising performances

At Brands Hatch for the next race AMR1/04, making its debut, was the sole Aston entry. Each successive AMR1 was lighter than the one before it and AMR1/04 also benefited from extensive suspension work which made it a much better-handling machine. Despite an ill-fitting seat, Leslie and Redman brought the Aston home a superb fourth, behind a Sauber-Mercedes and two Porsches, and ahead of the brand new turbocharged Jaguar XJR-11. But for a cockpit air vent coming adrift and costing the Aston a half-minute pit stop, the team could well have had a podium finish.

Carbon-fibre brakes were fitted for the next round, at the Nürburgring, where the AMR1's lack of top-end pace kept it down the field and the Leslie/Redman combination had to settle for eighth place. A two-car entry at Donington in September provided another solid result, Redman/Sears seventh in AMR1/04 just behind Leslie/Roe in the new (and even lighter) AMR1/05. Ahead of them were two Sauber-Mercedes, a Nissan, and two Porsches. Once again the Jaguar XJR-11 had been disappointing.

At Spa two weeks later misfires and tricky handling in the wet practice session left the Astons a long way down the grid, and then in the race the Leslie/Roe AMR1/05 broke a conrod while in eighth place. Redman and Stanley Dickens (winner at Le Mans earlier in the year in a Sauber-Mercedes) in AMR1/04 recovered from 32nd place on the grid to

Left *Neat AMR1 interior. Note the digital readouts on the dash.*

Below *Huge discs gave the AMR1 awesome stopping power, even by Group C standards.*

finish a fighting seventh. AMR1/05 was then fitted with a new 'Version II' 6.3-litre engine and dispatched to Mexico for the final round of the championship, where Leslie and Redman finished eighth after being held up by slower cars for much of the race. Meanwhile, TWR finally managed a result by wheeling out the old V12 Jaguar XJR-9s, finishing fifth and sixth with a bit of help from two pace-car periods. Aston Martin ended the year with sixth place in the World Sports Prototype Championship, a good effort for a debut year.

Work had already begun on a lighter, quicker AMR2 with a 'Version III' Callaway engine for 1990 when a shock announcement was made: Aston Martin would not race again and the Proteus team was being disbanded. Officially the reasons were that Le Mans looked in jeopardy for 1990 due to a battle over TV rights, and in any case the regulations would be changing for 1991 to require a 3.5-litre engine which Aston Martin could not afford to develop. Behind the scenes, it had been planned to produce an Aston Martin 'endurance' version of the Ford-Cosworth HB 75-degree V8 engine which was then winning in Benetton's Formula One chassis. But then Ford paid £1.6billion for Jaguar, suddenly the Cosworth engine was being sent to Coventry, and that meant the end of Aston Martin in racing.

Above *The Callaway-developed 32-valve engine developed around 700bhp.*

AMR1 was essentially a sound design, and once the handling had been sorted out its main problem was an excess of aerodynamic downforce and drag. If AMR2 had emerged as a lighter AMR1, with less drag to help the top-end performance, it could have been a serious player in the 1990 championship. From Ford's point of view it might have taken the fight to the Mercedes team while TWR was still trying to sort the bugs out of its unreliable Jaguar XJR-11s. The Cosworth engine would have been a relatively cheap way of taking Aston Martin sports cars into 1991, and could easily have made Aston Martin a winner. That same engine would instead power Ross Brawn's Jaguar XJR-14 chassis to victory in the 1991 World Sportscar Championship. Aston enthusiasts could only watch from the sidelines and wonder what might have been.

Ford and the V-Cars

For the 1990s Aston Martin needed a brand new car, but replacing the Aston Martin V8 saloon would be no easy task. The big Aston had been in production in one form or another since the late 1960s. As far back as 1976, when William Towns' Lagonda looked like it was the shape of things to come, there had been thoughts about phasing out the old Aston. But time after time it had proved the doubters wrong and every time it had been upgraded and improved, buyers had queued up for the new version. Whatever was to replace it would have a tough act to follow.

The new car not only had to deliver the performance expected of an Aston, it also had to be capable of meeting increasingly tight exhaust emissions and safety laws – preferably without needing different specifications for different territories, as was the case with the current V8. It had to be cheaper and easier to build, and far more modern in technology and appearance – but at the same time it had to retain Aston Martin's traditional hand-built fit and finish, to avoid alienating Aston's legion of satisfied serial owners. And it had to have styling with a timeless quality that could last well through the decade, or perhaps even longer.

While the Vantage Zagato was holding press and public attention, work was already beginning behind the scenes to provide the new mainstream Aston with a clean, powerful and efficient engine by using four-valve cylinder heads. Four small valves can offer better gas-flow than two large ones, also allowing the spark plug to be positioned in the centre instead of off to one side – all of which improves combustion efficiency, which can boost the power output and at the same time help reduce fuel consumption and exhaust emissions. Four tiny valves are also lighter than two thumping great big ones, and the reduction in valvetrain inertia allows higher revs to be used reliably, and reduces wear. The big Aston engine, with its huge valves, was an ideal candidate for the four-valve treatment.

Many of Aston's development staff had left to form the company's engineering subsidiary Aston Martin Tickford, which was hived off into a separate company in 1983 (eventually becoming part of David Richards' Prodrive group in 2001). Outside assistance was needed to develop the revised engine and it came in the shape of Callaway Engineering, run by former racer Reeves Callaway. The Connecticut-based company had considerable experience of four-valve-per-cylinder-head design and in April 1986, a month after Aston Martin showed the 432bhp Vantage Zagato in public for the first time, Callaway began the task of redesigning the Tadek Marek V8 to use four-valve cylinder heads. Hydraulic tappets were also incorporated in the design to reduce maintenance requirements. The bottom end, which had proved to be very reliable in the road cars and in the racing engines, was unchanged.

A few weeks later, Aston Martin invited five designers to put forward styling proposals for the new car, and these were evaluated as quarter-scale models in August 1986: the winning design was by John Heffernan and Ken Greenley, vehicle design tutors at the Royal College of Art. The new shape was very modern, yet of a more ageless style than William Towns' Lagonda, which had seemed so advanced in 1976 but which had dated very rapidly – soon Towns would be engaged on the restyle that would soften the big saloon's sharp edges. The Heffernan/Greenley Aston was altogether curvier, combining an aggressive stance with an elegant and understated appearance. Though width and wheelbase were almost identical to the old V8 saloon, the new car was slightly longer to

Previous page 1993 Vantage with twin superchargers provided 550bhp performance.

Below The Callaway-developed four-valve cylinder head used on the Virage.

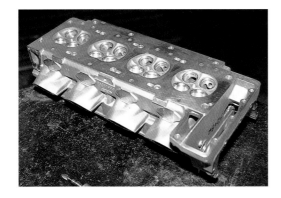

DB4GT Zagato 'Sanction II'

By the mid-1980s prices of rare and collectable cars had rocketed to levels never before seen. Limited edition models were being built to take advantage of the market – cars such as the Ferrari F40, Jaguar XJ220 and Aston's own Vantage Zagato – and the rarest and most sought-after classics were making record prices at auction.

One of the most revered and collectable cars of all was the DB4GT Zagato, of which just 19 were built between 1959 and 1962. In 1987, just prior to the takeover by Ford, Victor Gauntlett and Peter Livanos decided to build four new Zagatos to what was essentially the original 1960s specification. They would use four chassis numbers allocated in the 1960s, but never built. Four chassis were built up to DB4GT spec by Richard Williams, and then sent to Milan for Zagato to add the bodies. Alongside them was Williams' own original Zagato, which became the pattern for the new Zagato bodies.

Mirroring the production of the original Zagatos, the Sanction II cars were returned to England for completion, though they were not finished until 1991, the AMR1 project having got in the way. They were almost impossible to distinguish from a 1960s Zagato, but close inspection would show that the Sanction IIs, all painted metallic green, were fitted with 15-inch wire wheels and radial tyres rather than 16-inch wires with cross-plies. The suspension was revised to suit the new tyres, and adjustable anti-roll bars fitted at both ends. Sensibly, each Sanction II was fitted with a modern battery and an alternator rather than a dynamo. Though the engine was the correct Marek six, with the rare and expensive DB4GT twin-plug head, it had been bored out to displace 4.2-litres compared to the original cars' 3.7-litres. Twin-choke Weber carburettors of a similar type to the originals were fitted to a manifold with longer intake runners to improve gas flow. As a result the Sanction II generated nearly 70bhp more than an original Zagato, and the new cars were altogether swifter.

Two spare bodyshells were also built at the time, but neither was used for 'spares' and the shells remained in storage for some years. Eventually Richard Williams approached Walter Hayes for permission to build up the two cars and these 'Sanction III' Zagatos were completed in 1996. Several DB4s have been rebodied in the Zagato style over the years, but since the end of Zagato production in 1962 only these six Sanction II and Sanction III cars can claim to be 'the real thing'.

Left A 'Sanction II' Zagato built in 1991.

improve its aerodynamics, and there were hints of DB4 in its proportions. It looked, in fact, like an Aston – but a thoroughly modern one.

Under the sleek new skin the chassis was a development of that in the Lagonda saloon, itself a revised version of the V8's platform, with suspension which was similar in layout to the old cars' but different in detail. At the front the wishbones were retained, but the geometry altered. At the back the de Dion 'tube' was now a light alloy casting, and it was located fore and aft by cast alloy arms meeting at a large, rubber-mounted ball-joint under the back seat. A development 'mule' built to test the new chassis was fitted with a curious two-door version of the Lagonda's wedge-shaped body. By early 1988 D972MKX was a

Right The Virage outside 'Sunnyside', the Aston Martin offices in Newport Pagnell.

Above A drophead Volante version of the Virage was planned from the start.

1989 Virage

Engine:	V8, twin-overhead-cam per bank, four valves per cylinder
Bore/stroke:	100mm x 85mm
Capacity:	5340cc
Power:	335bhp @ 5300rpm
Fuel system:	Weber/Marelli engine management
Gearbox:	5-speed ZF manual
Chassis:	Steel platform
Body:	Steel box-section body frame with aluminium alloy panels
Suspension:	Front: wishbones with coil springs and anti-roll bar. Rear: de Dion with coil springs, A-frame and Watt linkage
Brakes:	Discs all round (outboard rear)
Top speed:	157mph (253km/h)
Acceleration:	0-60mph (97km/h) in 6.8sec

familiar site around Newport Pagnell and at test venues such as Bruntingthorpe Proving Ground in Leicestershire. When *Motor* magazine spotted it, Victor Gauntlett told them he was starting to like the shape, and wondering if Aston Martin might be able to sell some…

New ownership

The new car – christened Virage, French for 'corner' or 'bend' – made its debut on the Aston Martin stand at the Birmingham International Motor Show in October 1988, where crowds of enthusiasts packed the gangways, all anxious to take a look at the new shape of Aston Martin and the first new Aston for a generation. The Virage was applauded for its styling, and it proved to be quieter and more comfortable than the old V8, though only a fraction faster because it had a similar power-to-weight ratio. Less happy were its road manners: the compliance in the rear suspension that helped to improve the ride also led to some criticisms of vagueness and instability in handling, and concerns about an excess of rear-end squat under acceleration. Even so, most buyers of the standard saloon probably preferred the more comfort-orientated chassis that was the result.

While development of the Virage had been in full swing, major changes had been happening behind the scenes at Aston Martin. Victor Gauntlett had been approached by Ford with a view to taking over the company. Although Gauntlett had weathered the economic crises of the early 1980s and had turned Aston Martin into a viable independent company, he could see that Newport Pagnell's future with Ford backing would be much more secure. As part of the Ford family, Aston Martin would be financially stronger, and would have a lot more clout with its suppliers. Sourcing components was a full-time job because manufacturers had to be persuaded to supply a few hundred units to Aston Martin every year, when they were more interested in supplying millions of components to the major car makers. Moreover, keeping up with global emissions and safety legislation was incredibly expensive; with Ford's backing, Aston Martins could be kept continually abreast of new regulations, opening up new world markets. Developing additional new models would also become a possibility, which might mean that Gauntlett's much-discussed 'DP1999', the new DB4, could become a reality. With all this in mind, Gauntlett

and Peter Livanos sold 75 per cent of Aston Martin to Ford on 7 September, 1987, splitting the rest of the shares between them. Ford's bosses asked Gauntlett himself to stay on as chairman for the time being.

With the release of the Virage, the old V8 saloon and Vantage were phased out, while the popular drophead Volante continued for a few more months. For the last few years of its production run the Volante had been available as a Vantage Volante, with the more powerful Vantage engine and wide wheel-arch extensions covering Vantage-specification wheels and tyres. On the Vantage Volante, however, the styling changes went further than just the wheel arches: the arch extensions at the front and rear were joined with glassfibre sill extensions to avoid stones being thrown up onto the bodywork by the wide wheels. A tall tail spoiler completed the package. It was certainly distinctive but didn't have the elegance normally expected of Aston Martin – it looked a little like a caricature. One distinguished customer certainly thought so: the Prince of Wales ordered his Vantage Volante with the Vantage engine but with standard Volante bodywork – apart from the Vantage bonnet, which was essential to clear the big Weber carburettors that were still part of the Vantage-spec engine. In the final few years of Volante production, a couple of dozen 'Prince of Wales spec' Vantage Volantes were built, cars which today are much sought-after by collectors.

A Volante version of the Virage had been planned right from the start, and it was launched at the next Birmingham Motor Show in 1990. Reaction was very positive, even though the Virage Volante had some drawbacks compared to the previous open Aston. For a start it was only a two-seater, with a luggage area behind the front seats, and it had a rather unsightly convertible hood which sat high above the line of the body when folded. The answer would come a couple of years later, with a 2+2 Volante featuring a much-improved hood, though even that lacked the elegance of the old V8 Volante.

After the Ford takeover Victor Gauntlett remained Aston Martin's chairman until 1991. He was succeeded by a familiar Ford face, Walter Hayes, who came out of retirement to take over at Newport Pagnell. Years before it had been Hayes who had brokered a deal between Ford, Lotus and Cosworth to build the DFV Grand Prix engine, which would go

Below The 32-valve engine was developed by Callaway in Connecticut.

Bottom Traditional appointments inside the Virage pleased Aston enthusiasts.

Above Walter Hayes took over the chairmanship of Aston Martin in 1991.

Above right The Virage Volante's hood never stowed away quite as neatly as on the previous V8 Volante.

Below While the Vantage was being developed, Aston Service tempted owners with this 465bhp, 6.3-litre engine conversion.

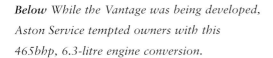

on to become the most successful Formula One engine of all time. Hayes, too, had been a major figure in Ford's involvement with rallying, which resulted in the RS Escorts that dominated the sport in the 1970s. Hayes had suggested to Henry Ford II that the Ford Motor Company should buy Aston Martin. As chairman, one of his first decisions was to sanction a new performance conversion being developed by Aston's service department.

Aston specialist Richard Williams had developed a 6.3-litre conversion for the Marek V8 engine several years earlier. The lessons learned from those road engines had gone into the 6.3-litre four-valve 'Version II' unit which raced just once in the Aston Martin AMR1 – which, of course, was managed by Williams. Once the Aston Group C project had ended, Williams went back to tuning the V8. By 1992 he was at work on a 7.0-litre version of the 16-valve V8 which produced around 500bhp. Meanwhile, Aston's service department had bought his 6.3-litre conversion and had now turned it into a production-ready kit for the Virage's 32-valve engine. Its bigger bores were filled with special Cosworth pistons, with H-section Carillo conrods acting on a forged-steel crankshaft with a longer stroke. The cylinder heads were reworked by Tickford to improve gas flow, and the engine management system's ignition and fuelling maps were revised. The 6347cc engine developed 465bhp, with 460lb ft of torque available at 4250rpm – quite a high engine speed, which might suggest that the 6.3's delivery was on the peaky side, until you find out that its torque curve was already heading rapidly for 400lb ft at a shade over 2000rpm.

Major upgrade

The Aston Service 6.3 was, however, far more than just an engine upgrade – as it should have been with a price tag of £60,000 (on top of the price of a Virage, of course). Gone was the faithful old ZF 5-speed gearbox, its place taken by a new 6-speeder from the same company – a gearbox previously seen in the Chevrolet Corvette ZR-1 and the 170mph (274km/h) Lotus Carlton. Stiffer springs and anti-roll bars were allied to Koni dampers, and some of the rubber suspension joints were replaced by steel spherical joints to sharpen up the handling. Braking was by huge AP Racing discs and the same calipers as Jaguar's XJ220 supercar, all controlled by an anti-lock system for the first time. To make space for

the brakes, the wheels were 10x18in OZ Racing split-rim alloys, and Goodyear produced a special batch of enormous 285/45ZR18 tyres similar in pattern to those used on the Corvette. Covering them were widened wheel arches which gave the 6.3 a much more aggressive stance than the standard Virage.

The result combined all the quality and opulence of the Virage with the kind of raw power not seen since the demise of the V8 Vantage nearly three years earlier. Indeed, performance figures were very similar to the V8 Vantage, as the 6.3's greater power balanced out the extra weight of the Virage's more luxurious appointments and higher level of equipment: the difference in weight was the equivalent of carrying a full complement of passengers. Compared to the standard Virage, the 6.3 could reach 60mph (97km/h) from rest more than a second quicker and it would go on to reach 100mph (161km/h) in under 13 seconds – three seconds ahead of the 5.3-litre Virage. Such was its performance that Aston Martin announced it would offer buyers the option of driver training at Goodwood, in the capable hands of former Grand Prix driver Peter Gethin.

Despite another economic downturn, the 6.3 proved to be a useful money-spinner for Aston Martin, as did another service department project, a £165,000 Shooting Brake. Rather than leave the estate conversion in the hands of a specialist coachbuilder, as they had done years before with the Harold Radford-built DB5 and DB6 Shooting Brakes, Aston Martin this time produced their own in-house conversion. Still capable of more than 150mph (241km/h), it must have been the fastest estate car on the planet, but despite the performance it still had a certain degree of practicality. Like lesser estate cars, it had a split, fold-down rear seat to increase the luggage capacity and a lift-up tailgate supported on gas struts. There was even a dog guard, and a fold-down flap to protect the back bumper while loading and unloading.

Top The 6.3 package also included running gear upgrades and bodywork modifications.

Above 10x18in OZ Racing wheels were fitted to the 6.3, with AP Racing discs inside them.

Top The production Shooting Brake suited the Virage's lines admirably.

Above The Virage Shooting Brake was surprisingly practical.

Vantage takes the limelight

Though the 6.3 received a lot of favourable press, it wasn't the ultimate expression of the Virage that everyone was waiting for. It was common knowledge that a Vantage version was being developed, and it broke cover at the Birmingham Motor Show in October 1992. The new Vantage's lines had been penned by John Heffernan, and the result had all the aggression of the 6.3 but wrapped in a more cohesive package. This time the front and rear of the car came in for considerable modification, as well as the sides. At the front, six small headlights sat behind flush-fitting plastic covers, and the under-bumper air dam was now larger and more extravagantly ducted. Above the new circular rear lights, the boot lid was extended to reduce lift over the rear axle, and indeed the Vantage was claimed to generate positive downforce at speed. Though the car's wider wings probably increased its frontal area compared to the Virage, a lower drag coefficient ensured that drag was kept to a minimum.

Beneath those wings were six-spoke alloy wheels carrying 285/45x18 Goodyear Eagle tyres, as seen on the 6.3, and revised suspension which at the rear reverted to the old V8's arrangement of twin trailing arms on each side. The de Dion axle's Watt link was retained to provide lateral location but instead of it being mounted at the centre of the axle it was now mounted centrally on the chassis, picking up on the axle at each end. The benefit was that this kept the rear roll centre at a constant height, which controlled weight transfer as the car cornered and improved the handling. The new suspension would soon be used on Virages too, though without the stiffer springs, dampers and anti-roll bars that were part of the Vantage specification. Bosch ABS was fitted, controlling all-disc brakes with 14-inch front discs – exactly the same set-up as the 6.3.

Ford's First Family

Though renowned for building cars for the masses, the Ford Motor Company has dallied with sports cars throughout its history, and has been competing in motor sport for more than 100 years. Henry Ford himself held the World Land Speed record for a couple of weeks in 1904, racing across Lake St Clair at 91.4mph (147.1km/h) in the famous Ford Arrow.

In the 1960s Ford president Lee Iacocca pushed to acquire Ferrari, and when the negotiations failed, he instead set Ford on the path to beat Ferrari at its own game, with the GT40. That done, Iacocca supported a move to buy into De Tomaso, which itself had just bought the troubled Ghia styling house. De Tomaso's Pantera sports car was intended to sell in huge numbers, though it never did; the silver lining was that when Ford and Alejandro De Tomaso split, Ford retained Ghia to act as a styling consultant.

In 1981 Bob Lutz, then running Ford of Europe, instigated the AC Ghia, a purposeful-looking sports car that might have become a rally competitor for Ford. Nothing ever came of it, though relations between Ford and AC would grow, Ford briefly supporting the company financially.

More long-lasting relationships were formed with Mazda (from 1979), Aston Martin (from 1987) and Jaguar (from 1989). Volvo was added to the portfolio of European brands in January 1999. Ford had already tried to buy Rover, with its eye on the profitable Land Rover marque. It got its chance in 2000 when BMW broke up the troubled Rover Group, and the deal included the technical centre at Gaydon in Warwickshire. Ford's uprange European marques – Aston Martin, Jaguar, Land Rover and Volvo – are now grouped together under the umbrella of the London-based Premier Automotive Group, initially run by former Rover Group boss Wolfgang Reitzle.

Jackie Stewart's Grand Prix team, partly funded by Ford from the start, was taken over completely in 1999 to form the basis of the so far unsuccessful Jaguar F1 effort. Pi Research and Cosworth Racing are also now wholly-owned subsidiaries, forming Ford's 'Premier Performance Division'. But Cosworth Technology, which builds the V12 engines for Aston Martin, is now owned by Audi.

Below Ford's Italian supercar, using Dearborn V8 engines – the DeTomaso Pantera.

Bottom left Jaguar's XJ220 was hurried into public view to try to steal the Virage's thunder.

Above The GT40 played Ferrari at its own game – and won.

1993 Vantage

Engine:	V8, twin-overhead-cam per bank, four valves per cylinder, twin Eaton superchargers
Bore/stroke:	100mm x 85mm
Capacity:	5340cc
Power:	550bhp @ 6500rpm
Fuel system:	Bosch injection with EEC IV management
Gearbox:	6-speed ZF manual
Chassis:	Steel platform
Body:	Steel box-section body frame with aluminium alloy panels
Suspension:	Front: wishbones with coil springs and anti-roll bar. Rear: de Dion with coil springs, trailing arms and Watt linkage
Brakes:	Discs all round (outboard rear), ABS
Top speed:	186mph (299km/h)
Acceleration:	0-60mph (97km/h) in 4.6sec

Above right The Vantage restyle was more harmonious than the 6.3, but just as aggressive.

Below Twin Eaton superchargers boosted the V8's power output to 550bhp.

Under the bonnet, though, things were very different to the 6.3, because the Vantage retained the 5340cc capacity that had been standard for the Marek engine since the DBS V8 of 1969. To boost power, Aston Martin turned to forced induction – but instead of using turbochargers, which had been a common solution for other manufacturers during the 1980s, they fitted two Roots-type Eaton superchargers delivering up to 10psi boost. Turbochargers are driven by exhaust gases, so they tend not to work very well at low engine speeds and small throttle openings when exhaust gas flow is slight. The result is a big step in the power curve as the revs build, and a delay in response when the throttle is snapped open – known as 'turbo lag'. Superchargers are driven directly from the engine, in this case by belts, improving the shape of the torque curve and giving much quicker response to the throttle. The drawback is that the superchargers are always being driven, so they use up power and fuel even when they are not required to do useful work. On the Vantage an air by-pass system was incorporated to recirculate low-pressure air into the superchargers to reduce the losses. Twin alloy intercoolers were fitted to keep intake air temperatures as low as possible to improve power and reliability.

As is normal with forced-induction engines, the 'geometric' compression ratio was reduced, to 8.2:1. The Weber/Marelli fuel injection system of the Virage was replaced by Bosch injection equipment controlled by Ford's powerful EEC IV engine management system, specially developed for the Vantage by Aston Martin. This treated each bank of cylinders as a separate four-cylinder engine and enabled the big V8 to pass all current and foreseeable emissions laws. In fact, under some circumstances the exhaust gases it emitted could be cleaner than the air entering the intakes. Power output under test conditions was 550bhp, though in common with all forced-induction engines a cold day would improve the intercooling and could liberate a little more horsepower. All that power was fed to the same 6-speed manual gearbox as had been used on the 6.3, with a closely-stacked set of intermediate gears and a very high sixth that left the Vantage engine spinning at little more than tickover at the British legal limit of 70mph (113km/h).

Whatever limit was imposed, getting there would not take long. The Vantage was, even by the standards of its forebears, blisteringly fast. Despite an all-up weight approaching two tons, the Vantage despatched the 0-60mph (97km/h) sprint in around 4.6 seconds, and if you kept your foot down 100mph (161km/h) would come up in a fraction over 10 seconds. The car had been timed at 186mph (299km/h), and there were suggestions that it was actually quicker than that. There were few rivals that could match that kind of pace. The new turbocharged Lotus Esprit SE could get close to the Aston's 0-60mph time, but not its top speed – and the Lotus was much less refined and nowhere near as well built. The Lamborghini Diablo, Ferrari's 512 Testarossa and Jaguar's XJ220 were all amazing machines that could match or exceed the Aston's speed, but none had accommodation for four people. Porsche's 911 Turbo was more practical than the Italians, but it lacked the Aston's exclusivity. Few other cars even came close.

Vantage reaction

Reaction to the Vantage was predictably enthusiastic, though there was some criticism of a jittery ride, fuel consumption which only just struggled into double figures, and the ugly Ford-sourced airbag-equipped steering wheel. Even so, *Autocar* said the Vantage was proof that Aston Martin was again doing what it did best, building 'quintessentially British road burners'. Jeremy Clarkson, Britain's most outspoken motoring critic, spent three days with a Vantage and, after discovering it had enough power to spin its wheels on a dry road at more than 90mph (145km/h), told *Performance Car* readers that it was 'the most wonderful car in the world'.

The Vantage certainly generated the right sort of publicity for Aston Martin, though it was the Volante, now in revised 2+2 form, which was the mainstay of production at Newport Pagnell. But in spite of a worldwide recession, there would always be customers with money to spend on bespoke motor cars, and orders continued to come in for 6.3 conversions – now being applied to the Volante as well as to the Virage saloon. Some customers also asked for 'cosmetic' 6.3s, with the revised bodywork but without the engine modifications, and the service department was happy to oblige. Towards the end of 1993 Aston's service department offered two more conversions, engineered by Mike Loasby and this time focusing on the Virage's body rather than its engine. Offering them

Above Lagonda returned in 1993 with four-door saloon and Shooting Brake conversions by Newport Pagnell's service department.

Left The long-wheelbase Volante answered criticisms about lack of rear legroom.

149

1996 V8 Coupé

Engine:	V8, twin-overhead-cam per bank, four valves per cylinder
Bore/stroke:	100mm x 85mm
Capacity:	5340cc
Power:	350bhp @ 6500rpm
Fuel system:	Weber Alpha Plus engine management
Gearbox:	5-speed ZF manual or 4-speed automatic
Chassis:	Steel platform
Body:	Steel box-section body frame with aluminium alloy panels
Suspension:	Front: wishbones with coil springs and anti-roll bar. Rear: de Dion with coil springs, trailing arms and Watt linkage
Brakes:	Discs all round (outboard rear), ABS
Top speed:	'Over 150mph' (241km/h)
Acceleration:	0-60mph (97km/h) in 'under 6.0sec'

Above right The first of the 10 Limited Edition Coupés.

Below The V8 Coupé's styling was based on the Vantage.

as conversions, rather than new models, avoided costly Type Approval testing, but even then these weren't cheap cars. For £115,000 your Virage could be lengthened and a second set of doors added to turn it into a rather handsome notchback four-door saloon. The roof was also raised slightly to improve rear-seat headroom. Another £6000 could turn your Virage into a five-door Shooting Brake with a third row of seats to make it a seven-seater. Both conversions were given Lagonda badges, the four-door saloon effectively replacing the William Towns Lagonda which had been quietly phased out in 1990.

New coupé

The release of the successful Vantage and the DB7 (which has its own chapter) at either end of the Aston spectrum led to a fall in demand for the standard Virage saloon in the middle. A Limited Edition model announced in October 1994 would be the final model with a Virage badge, and boasted a 10 per cent power increase, anti-lock brakes, British Racing Green paintwork and an attractive mesh grille. For a while Newport Pagnell concentrated on Vantages and Volantes, but in March 1996, at the Geneva show, a new mid-range V8 model was announced. The £149,500 'V8 Coupé' was essentially a normally-aspirated version of the Vantage, with a revised 350bhp version of the four-valve V8. Its bodywork was very slightly less wild as the arches were required to cover wheels 'only' 8.5 inches wide instead of the Vantage's enormous 10x18in rims. As before manual and automatic gearboxes were available, with the majority of customers opting for the four-speed, dual-mode automatic. At the London show the following year Aston Martin unveiled a 'Vantage-look' Volante on a 10-inch (254mm) longer wheelbase than the Coupé and Vantage, which gave better rear-seat legroom although it lacked the torsional stiffness of the shorter Volante.

In 1998 Project Vantage wowed motor show crowds the world over, and revealed the future direction of Aston Martin design. Clearly the time of the 'V cars', as the Virage and its derivatives had become known, would soon be over. But there was still more to come from the big Newport Pagnell Astons. As a step beyond its 6.3 conversion, Aston Martin's service department – now called Works Service – developed a 600bhp version of the Vantage engine. The extra power was derived from higher boost pressure, better intercooling and a freer-flowing exhaust system, and it pushed the Vantage's top speed to around the 200mph (322km/h) mark – provided you could find a road long enough, straight enough and empty enough to give it a try. Options included Dymag magnesium alloy wheels, AP Racing brakes, Stack digital instrumentation of the type used in racing cars, and revised suspension with adjustable dampers, higher-rated springs and stiffer anti-roll bars.

A special edition Le Mans Vantage was announced in 1999, celebrating the 40th anniversary of Aston Martin's Le Mans win. Available with either the 'standard' 550bhp Vantage engine or the 'Works Prepared' 600bhp unit, the Le Mans Vantage was distinguished by its bigger front air dam, partially blanked-off grille aperture and DBR1-style side vents. Just 40 cars were built, one for each year, Aston's own demonstrator being painted the same metallic racing green the works team had used in the 1950s. The following year a batch of just eight Volante 600s was built, on the stiffer short-wheelbase platform, with the 600bhp engine and Le Mans Vantage styling.

The last V8 was built in October 2000 and it marked the end of an era – the end of a family of cars which could trace its lineage as far back as the DB4 of 1958. The end, too, of the much-developed Harold Beach platform chassis and the much-modified Tadek Marek V8, as neither would feature in Aston Martin's forthcoming models. It was the end, in fact, of a whole generation of bespoke, aluminium-bodied Aston Martins. Newport Pagnell had made just over 5000 V8 Astons, and would again make cars of great distinction, combining immense power and performance with the finest quality and luxury. But they would never be quite the same again.

Above 'Works Prepared' Vantage had 600bhp.

Below left Interior of the Le Mans Vantage, released in 1999 to mark the 40th anniversary of Aston Martin's Le Mans victory.

1999 Vantage Le Mans

Engine:	V8, twin-overhead-cam per bank, four valves per cylinder, twin Eaton superchargers
Bore/stroke:	100mm x 85mm
Capacity:	5340cc
Power:	600bhp @ 6750rpm
Fuel system:	Bosch injection with EEC IV management
Gearbox:	6-speed ZF manual
Chassis:	Steel platform
Body:	Steel box-section body frame with aluminium alloy panels
Suspension:	Front: wishbones with coil springs and anti-roll bar. Rear: de Dion with coil springs, trailing arms and Watt linkage
Brakes:	Discs all round (outboard rear), ABS
Top speed:	Over 200mph (322km/h)
Acceleration:	0-60mph (97km/h) in 4.0sec

DB Returns

Above The DB7 was styled by Ian Callum, seen here with the 1998 Project Vantage concept – another Callum design.

Previous page 2001 DB7 Vantage Volante.

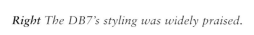

Above Testing in the Arctic Circle. The DB7 was the most rigorously developed Aston yet.

Right The DB7's styling was widely praised.

V̲ictor Gauntlett's dream of building a 'new DB4' alongside the big V8 Astons finally came to fruition under Ford's ownership. Aston Martin needed a car that would, in its terms, be a volume seller. The expensive V8s were dependent on a buoyant economy for customers, and the worldwide recession had slowed production to a trickle, with just 46 cars made in 1991. But as the new chairman Walter Hayes could see, producing a smaller and cheaper Aston in much larger numbers than had previously been possible meant more than just designing a new car. It meant finding somewhere to build the new machine and restructuring the whole company to cope with new production methods and a whole new ethos. The changes wrought by the decision to build a small Aston would be far-reaching.

For a start the new Aston, codenamed NPX, could not be built at Newport Pagnell. Though the famous old factory, either side of Tickford Street in the small Buckinghamshire village, was perfectly satisfactory for producing small numbers of hand-built cars – just one or two a week during the troubled early 1990s – it lacked both the space and the organization to cope with a 12-cars-a-week production line. Ford's takeover of Jaguar offered a solution: TWR, on Jaguar's behalf, was building a short run of XJ220s at a new factory in Bloxham, near Oxford. Once that production run was complete, NPX could take over the facility and although production would necessarily be more mechanized than was the case at Newport Pagnell the cars would still be essentially hand-made.

TWR was also heavily involved in the development of the new car, and the Jaguar connection would provide the starting point. Ford had cancelled Jaguar's F-Type project shortly after buying the company, reasoning that it was too expensive to make in the kind of numbers that would be necessary for Jaguar. As an Aston, however, volumes would be lower and prices could be higher – and suddenly the project made sense. So NPX was derived from Jaguar's stillborn F-Type, itself based on a modified version of the highly accomplished XJS platform. Early development cars also used XJS bodyshells, with strange bubble arches to cater for the new car's wider track.

Above The DB7 had a lot of Jaguar engineering under the skin.

Left TWR's Neil Simpson designed the interior.

Power for the new car would also derive from a Jaguar source, rather than from Newport Pagnell's venerable V8. NPX would have a straight-six engine based on Jaguar's AJ6 unit, though in Aston form the 3.2-litre motor had a new cylinder head and an Eaton supercharger. Normally aspirated, the engine was good for just over 200bhp, but the modifications employed for its new application took the power output to a healthy 335bhp. Thanks to Walter Hayes' unmatched range of contacts, the new car's ride and handling were fettled by no less a driver than the three-times World Champion Jackie Stewart, who had become an Aston director.

NPX's body was another departure from the Aston Martin norm. Instead of using Aston's traditional bodywork material, aluminium alloy, NPX had a steel body with composite bonnet, boot lid, sills and front wings. The shape was created by Ian Callum, who had been recruited to TWR from the Ford-owned Ghia design house. The curvaceous shape that Callum drew was unlike anything yet seen on an Aston, and yet it had the right kind of feel to it. It incorporated Aston styling cues – the DB3S grille shape and the wing vent, and there were hints of DB4GT Zagato – within a modern aerodynamic shape. However, the critics would argue that it had more than a hint of Jaguar about it. But most people who saw it liked it, and indeed there were many who were prepared to claim it was the prettiest shape they'd seen in many a year. There was some disquiet about the large 'aero' hubcaps, behind which sat rather elegant multi-spoke alloy wheels, though the word was that they were fitted to hide the rather feeble-looking Jaguar brakes. To complement the curvaceous exterior, TWR's Neil Simpson created an equally sinuous cabin clad in Connolly leather, with space for two adults and two smallish children. In this form NPX made its public debut at the Geneva show in March 1993, and despite the announcements of Bugatti's EB112 saloon concept and Ferrari's 348 Spider, the new Aston Martin DB7 stole the show. The revival of the famous DB model line coincided with the return of 'DB' himself, Sir David Brown, who was invited to become the company's President.

1993 DB7	
Engine:	In-line six, twin-overhead-cam per bank, four valves per cylinder, supercharged
Bore/stroke:	91mm x 83mm
Capacity:	3228cc
Power:	335bhp @ 5500rpm
Fuel system:	Ford EEC V engine management
Gearbox:	5-speed Getrag manual, optional 4-speed automatic
Chassis/body:	Steel monocoque body/chassis, with composite bumpers, sills, front wings and boot lid
Suspension:	Front: wishbones with coil springs and anti-roll bar. Rear: wishbones with coil springs and anti-roll bar
Brakes:	Ventilated discs all round, with Teves anti-lock
Top speed:	165mph (266km/h)
Acceleration:	0-60mph (97km/h) in 5.6sec

Above Aston Martin launched the DB7 Volante
in 1996.

Above The V12 engine used in the DB7
Vantage was loosely based on two Ford V6s.

Right The V12 made its debut in the Ford
Indigo show car of 1996.

Plenty of work was still to be done to the DB7 before it was ready for production, planned for April 1994. Over a million miles of testing took the 30 prototype cars to Arizona for high temperatures, Colorado for high altitude, and Ontario for low temperatures, in addition to the roads around TWR's Kidlington base. Detail changes were many, but the DB7's wonderful shape hardly altered – just about the only visible external change was the deletion of the removable roof panel that had been a feature of the show car (a sunroof was offered as an option). The result was the most thoroughly developed Aston yet, though it had taken longer than planned: production did not begin until the end of 1994 – ironically just at the time that Jaguar announced that it, too, would be using an Eaton-supercharged AJ6 engine, in the new XJR performance saloon.

With the DB7, as with the Virage before it, a drophead version had been planned right from the start of development. At the Detroit and Los Angeles auto shows in January 1996 Aston Martin launched the DB7 Volante and celebrated the new availability of the fixed-head DB7 in America, a vital export market. There were celebrations, too, for Aston Martin's best year of production ever – in 1995 more than 650 DB7s had been built at the

new Bloxham factory, and Newport Pagnell had added 100 Virages to the total. The same year had seen a racing DB7 with a 6.3-litre Richard Williams V8 under the bonnet fail to qualify for Le Mans by a slender margin, and three stripped-out racing 'DB7 GTs' were built by Prodrive and Works Service for a proposed DB7 racing series that never happened. Another V8 DB7 would surface in 1996, a road car built for an Aston enthusiast by Works Service and offering significantly more power and performance than standard.

Development of an 'official' solution for greater performance had begun in 1997, and arrived in public at the London Motor Show in 1999 with the launch of the DB7 Vantage and Vantage Volante. Early rumours had suggested the Vantage would use the AJ16, Jaguar's latest straight-six engine, again with a bespoke Aston cylinder head and an Eaton supercharger to raise power to around 400bhp. But the DB7 Vantage that appeared in 1999 was far more exciting, because it had an entirely new engine that was all its own. In a departure from the Aston norm that new engine was not a straight six or a V8 but a V12, which had been shown in mock-up form at the Turin show in 1994 and then as a running engine in the Ford Indigo show car of 1996, which was, despite its name, red. Indigo was a curious open-wheeled sports car which looked like a single-seater racer, but was much fatter and with two side-by-side seats. Ford design chief Jack Telnac had said the idea was to create a car that was impossible to ignore and Ford certainly achieved that, though whether people stopped and stared for the right reasons is debatable.

Bespoke V12

Though the engine concept was loosely based on two Ford Duratec V6s (the Ford Mondeo/Taurus unit) laid end to end, to dismiss it as a result would be to sell it short, as almost all the componentry in the new 60-degree V12 was specific to that engine. Cosworth cast the aluminium alloy heads and cylinder block in the same limited-production foundry in Worcester which is responsible for Ford's V10 Formula One engine and V8 IndyCar units. The block's deep-skirted design gave the V12 similar torsional stiffness to the Duratec V6 despite being twice as long. The heads retained the Duratec's combustion chamber, exhaust port design and four-valve layout – four-valve heads were now almost universal among performance engines, so the new Aston V12 (known to Cosworth as the SGA) was a 48-valve engine. Continuing an Aston tradition which dated back to the 1940s, the engine had twin camshafts per cylinder bank. Dimensions were 'oversquare' with an 89mm bore and 79.5mm stroke, allowing the 5.9-litre engine to run happily at 7000rpm. Ford's powerful Visteon engine management system, able to process 1.6 million commands per second, not only looked after fuelling and ignition but also monitored every cylinder on every revolution to check for successful combustion. Correct combustion creates ionized gas, which allows current to flow between the spark plug tips when a small voltage is applied after the main spark. If a spark plug was fouled or poor fuel caused detonation, the system could react by cutting off the fuel supply to the cylinder for a moment, preventing unburnt fuel escaping through the exhaust system to the detriment of the catalytic convertors and the environment. More importantly to the headline writers and, probably, the customer, the new engine developed 420bhp and turned the DB7 from swift to searingly fast: the top speed went up to 185mph (298km/h) and the 0-60mph (97km/h) time dropped to just under five seconds.

Above DB7 Vantages and Vantage Volantes soon accounted for the majority of DB7 sales.

2000 DB7 Vantage	
Engine:	V12, twin-overhead-cam per bank, four valves per cylinder
Bore/stroke:	89mm x 79.5mm
Capacity:	5935cc
Power:	420bhp @ 6000rpm
Fuel system:	Ford Visteon EEC V engine management
Gearbox:	6-speed manual, optional 5-speed automatic
Chassis/body:	Steel monocoque body/chassis, with composite bumpers, sills, front wings and boot lid
Suspension:	Front: wishbones with coil springs and anti-roll bar. Rear: wishbones with coil springs and anti-roll bar
Brakes:	Ventilated discs all round, cross-drilled at front, with Teves anti-lock
Top speed:	185mph (298km/h)
Acceleration:	0-60mph (97km/h) in 5.0sec

Ghia's Lagonda

At Geneva in March 1993 there was more Aston Martin news than just the launch of the DB7, as if that wasn't enough. Ghia exhibited a Lagonda show car, badged as a Vignale to avoid any confusion with Ghia-model Fords, for which the Italian brand was best known in Europe.

The Lagonda Vignale shape was by Moray Callum, brother of DB7 designer Ian and now design chief at Mazda, another Ford outpost. Combining bold curves and striking proportions, the Vignale was fresh and exciting, though some stopped short of calling it handsome. Oddly, like the DB7, it too had a touch of Jaguar about it: there were hints of 1960s Mk2 and MkX, particularly at the back. Ten years on,

Mercedes' new Maybach exhibits some similar proportions. Inside, the Lagonda Vignale was equally eye-catching, with an amazing Art Deco interior full of leather and chrome, with an oval dashboard in stained beech.

Based on the extruded aluminium frame design that had been seen on the 1991 Ford Contour show car the Vignale was a running car, powered by a Lincoln Town Car V8 engine. The rumours were that a production version of the Lagonda, to be built at an expanded Bloxham factory, might get a 'modular' V12 engine that could save fuel by running on six or eight cylinders when full power was not needed. The aluminium frame could have been

retained, or the car adapted to use the Jaguar 'X300' platform.

Production of the Lagonda Vignale did look likely at one point – Moray Callum restyled it to be shorter and lower for production – but sadly it never happened. The show car was one of 51 Ford concepts sold by Christie's in 2002, the proceeds being donated to charity. The Vignale made more than $400,000. Apart from a few modified Virages built by Aston Works Service, no new Lagondas have been created since William Towns' wedge-shaped saloon quietly died in 1990. Although the Lagonda flag still flies at Newport Pagnell, only time will tell if the famous old marque will reappear.

Above *Amazing 'Art Deco' interior.*

Left *The Vignale, styled by Ian Callum's brother Moray, nearly made it into production.*

Major modifications were made to the rest of the car. Both the floor and the transmission tunnel had to be modified to fit the new V12 and its choice of transmissions, either the Tremec 6-speed manual used in the Chrysler Viper and Chevrolet Corvette or a 5-speed automatic shared with BMW's 7-series and the Rolls-Royce Silver Seraph. At the same time the structure was stiffened to aid handling and remove any possibility of scuttle-shake from the Volante version. Both the front and rear suspensions were heavily revised, the front receiving new wishbones and a new vertical link to reduce steering offset, while a cruciform brace was added under the rear axle to reduce axle tramp. Stiffer springs were

used all round, along with Bilstein dampers offering greater control of both bump and rebound, and the steering was sharpened from 2.7 to 2.5 turns lock to lock. Curiously, the Vantage's front wheels and tyres – 8-inch wide rims with 245/40ZR18 Bridgestones – were the same size as the standard DB7, though the rear wheels were an inch wider and carried 265/35ZR18 rubber. Alternatively, 19-inch wheels with incredibly low profile Yokohama tyres (245/35 front, 265/30 rear) were available as an option. Despite the massive tyres used even in standard specification, the engine management system incorporated a traction control facility which could react in just 64 milliseconds, throttling back the engine and, if necessary, applying the rear brakes to quell wheelspin.

Vantage restyle

Bigger cooling air intakes were incorporated into the nose and Ian Callum relocated the indicators and foglamps into a combination lamp unit, the shape and location of which was inspired by the Aston Martin racers of 40 years earlier. Initially wary of fiddling with his successful DB7 design, Callum was won over to the need for a restyle by the DB7 Vantage's much greater performance and the requirement for the larger intakes, which allowed him to rectify his only criticism of the DB7 shape, which was that the grille was too small in proportion to the rest of the car. In addition to the work on the front end, the sills were reshaped to make the DB7 Vantage look closer to the ground, and new wheels designed with ten thin, blade-like spokes to show off the huge cross-drilled Brembo brake discs and their Aston Martin-badged calipers. Though the family resemblance to the six-cylinder car was clear, the DB7 Vantage's shape shared elements with the Project Vantage show car which had been revealed a year earlier – though Ian Callum had completed it after the DB7 Vantage had been signed off. Inside the DB7 Vantage there were new seats with greater travel, new instruments, steering wheel and switches, and right-hand-drive cars gained a driver's foot rest.

Top and above Ian Callum subtly reworked the DB7's styling for the Vantage models.

Right The DB7 Vantage models – this is the drophead Volante – featured many interior improvements.

Below The Alfred Dunhill DB7's interior even included a humidor for storing cigars.

Right The Alfred Dunhill DB7.

Like the six-cylinder car, the DB7 Vantage had been subjected to rigorous development, despite a relatively short two-year gestation period. Prototypes covered half a million miles, including a 48-hour test running almost non-stop at 165mph (266km/h). At MIRA (Motor Industry Research Association) the cars were subjected to a 30-day accelerated durability test, said to be the equivalent of 100,000 miles (161,000km) of normal motoring, during which they were driven day and night at speeds from 1mph to 140mph (1.6-225km/h), and even deliberately driven into kerbstones at 50mph.

The Vantage helped Aston Martin to break all its production and sales records, as did special edition cars (designed in partnership with the respected Alfred Dunhill and Nieman Marcus brands) and even an appearance in the Sony Playstation game Gran Turismo. The DB7 quickly beat the previous record for the largest production of any single Aston model, which had been held by the DB6 since 1970. The 2000th DB7 was built at Bloxham in

June 1998, the 4000th in February 2000. Both cars were green, which accounts for 35 per cent of DB7 orders, with 25 per cent of customers requesting blue and 12 per cent opting for silver. More than a thousand new owners took delivery in 1999, the first time annual Aston Martin production had entered four figures, and all this from the same company that had taken 70 years to build its first 10,000 cars. Aston Martin also revealed that in 1999 DB7s had been supplied in nearly 100 different body colours, and that nearly half the cars built were then fettled by the service department at Newport Pagnell. Works Service offered a range of enhancements for the customer who wanted a more individual DB7, from V8 Vantage-style rear lights, alternative wheels and a racing-style starter button to bigger intercoolers, sports exhausts, V8 Vantage brakes and Rose-jointed adjustable suspension. The performance modifications were directly related to work that had gone into the DB7GT racing car project in 1995.

Death of the six

The six-cylinder DB7 remained available alongside the Vantage, but the price difference between the two was so small that more than 90 per cent of customers opted for the V12. By 2001 the six had disappeared. In January that year Aston Martin announced a new 'Touchtronic' control system for the DB7 Vantage's automatic gearbox, which gave the driver the facility to change manually up and down using plus and minus buttons on the steering wheel – similar to the system used in Formula One cars. At the Geneva Salon a few weeks later, ItalDesign showed a 500bhp DB7-based roadster called the Twenty Twenty, a curious design with exposed aluminium structural members and carbon-fibre panels. For the rest of that year all eyes were on the new Vanquish (see chapter 11) but a plan was in hand to return the DB7 to the limelight, with a new phase in Aston Martin's partnership with Zagato. By now the famous Italian coachbuilder was being run by

Above The DB7 broke all Aston Martin's production records – this is the 1000th car.

Below ItalDesign's DB7-based Twenty Twenty was Giugiaro's idea of an Aston for the future.

Above Interior of the Twenty Twenty concept.

Below right The DB7 Zagato made its bow at the Geneva show in 2002. Note the single grille, in place of the DB7's smaller twin intakes.

2002 DB7 GT

Engine:	V12, twin-overhead-cam per bank, four valves per cylinder
Bore/stroke:	89mm x 79.5mm
Capacity:	5935cc
Power:	435bhp @ 6000rpm
Fuel system:	Ford Visteon EEC V engine management
Gearbox:	6-speed manual, optional 5-speed automatic
Chassis/body:	Steel monocoque body/ chassis, with composite bumpers, sills, front wings and boot lid
Suspension:	Front: wishbones with coil springs and anti-roll bar. Rear: wishbones with coil springs and anti-roll bar
Brakes:	Grooved ventilated discs all round, with Teves anti-lock
Top speed:	Over 185mph (298km/h)
Acceleration:	0-60mph (97km/h) in 4.8sec

founder Udo Zagato's grandson Andrea, who met the new chairman of Aston Martin Lagonda, Dr Ulrich Bez, at the Pebble Beach Concours d'Elegance 2001. Soon the idea was formed to relaunch the collaboration between the two companies. Four months later, in January 2002, Zagato presented his first sketches of the car to Ulrich Bez and Aston Martin's new design director Henrik Fisker.

At the Geneva show in March the official announcement was made that a DB7 Zagato show car was being built, and that a short production run would follow if there was enough interest from customers. 'This could be anything between 75 and 99 cars depending on what our clients tell us,' Dr Bez told the press. 'We are anticipating a really positive reaction to the car and so far we have received a lot of interest and support.' Such was the interest, in fact, that a run of 99 cars was sanctioned and every one was sold before production began in 2003. As with previous Aston Zagato models, production was split between Italy and Britain: the DB7 Zagato bodies were built in Italy, then sent to Bloxham for final assembly.

The car that appeared differed somewhat from the original sketches, with longer overhangs, differences in the wing air vents and window line, and a less pronounced 'snout'. But the production DB7 Zagato was nevertheless a striking machine, and retained most of the ideas from the original drawings. In contrast to the DB7 Vantage's twin air intakes in its nose, the Zagato incorporated a large, single air intake, recalling the DB4GT Zagato of the 1960s, as did the muscular wheel arches and the shape of the glass area. The 'double bubble' roof that had become a Zagato trademark was extended backwards into a remarkable 'double bubble' rear window, turning the back of the car into a confluence of exciting curves.

There was more excitement under the skin. Tweaks to the V12 engine's management system liberated a few more horsepower, up from 420bhp to 435bhp. Overall gearing was lowered by fitting a shorter final drive, and the manual gearbox was given a quick-shift linkage. Overall weight dropped by 132lb (60kg) through wider use of aluminium alloy

for the body panels and a reduction in length of 211mm (about 8in). Overhangs front and rear were shorter and the Zagato's wheelbase was a fraction less than the DB7 Vantage's, but different offsets for the Zagato-styled 18-inch wheels gave the new car a slightly wider track. No performance figures were quoted, but the lighter weight and shorter gearing should have improved acceleration and top speed was also expected to improve.

Zagato performance

Perhaps some idea of the Zagato's performance potential could be gained from a new 435bhp version of the DB7 announced at the Birmingham Motor Show in October 2002. Called the DB7GT – the 1995 racing car project of the same name being deemed too obscure and too far back in time to cause any confusion – the new car offered a sportier interpretation of the DB7 Vantage theme, available in manual (GT) and automatic (GTA) forms. The most obvious changes were the new five-spoke 18-inch wheels and the anodized wire mesh air intakes at the front, plus new bonnet vents. Subtler changes included revisions to the underbody and a reshaped boot lid, which cut aerodynamic lift by half. A twin-plate clutch with an aluminium cover gave a greater friction area and reduced pedal effort by a fifth. A version of the Vanquish's active exhaust system was fitted, giving the GT low back-pressure at high engine speeds while still passing stringent drive-by noise regulations. Detail changes to the suspension and steering further sharpened the handling. The DB7GT used the Zagato's 435bhp engine and lower final drive ratio, and the result was a 0-60mph (97km/h) sprint time around 4.8 seconds and a top speed in excess of the DB7 Vantage's 185mph (298km/h).

Both the Zagato and the GT were made available only as fixed-head coupés, but the latest addition to the DB7 family redresses the balance for open-car enthusiasts. Originally there was some suggestion that the car would be called a Speedster, but when it was announced in January 2003 the new car carried the cumbersome title of 'DB American Roadster 1', or DB AR1. Though Aston Martin was keen to distance it from the Zagato, it

Above The DB7 Zagato is particularly successful from the rear. Note the 'double bubble' roof.

Below left Aston Martin announced the 435bhp DB7GT in 2002.

2003 DB7 Zagato

Engine:	V12, twin-overhead-cam per bank, four valves per cylinder
Bore/stroke:	89mm x 79.5mm
Capacity:	5935cc
Power:	435bhp @ 6000rpm
Fuel system:	Ford Visteon EEC V engine management
Gearbox:	6-speed manual, optional 5-speed automatic
Chassis/body:	Steel monocoque with aluminium outer panels
Suspension:	Front: wishbones with coil springs and anti-roll bar. Rear: wishbones with coil springs and anti-roll bar
Brakes:	Ventilated discs all round, cross-drilled at front, with Teves anti-lock
Top speed:	Over 185mph (298km/h)
Acceleration:	0-60mph (97km/h) in 4.8sec

2003 DB AR1

Engine:	V12, twin-overhead-cam per bank, four valves per cylinder
Bore/stroke:	89mm x 79.5mm
Capacity:	5935cc
Power:	435bhp @ 6000rpm
Fuel system:	Ford Visteon EEC V engine management
Gearbox:	6-speed manual, optional 5-speed automatic
Chassis/body:	Steel monocoque with aluminium outer panels
Suspension:	Front: wishbones with coil springs and anti-roll bar. Rear: wishbones with coil springs and anti-roll bar
Brakes:	Ventilated discs all round, cross-drilled at front, with Teves anti-lock
Top speed:	185mph (298km/h)
Acceleration:	0-60mph (97km/h) in 'under 5.0sec'

Above right DB AR1 production was limited to just 99 cars – all sold before production began.

Right The DB AR1 was designed for the dry states of the USA – there was no hood.

Opposite below The luxuriously appointed interior of the DB AR1.

had much in common. Engine and transmission were the same, the body shared the coupé's wide-mouthed styling and would again be built by Zagato, using the same construction method. Like the Zagato, the DB AR1's production run would be limited to just 99 cars. The main difference was that DB AR1 was a true roadster, with no hood, designed for the dry roads of California. Production is exclusively for America, the 99 customers each paying around $230,000 for one of the most exclusive variations on the DB7's highly successful theme.

Another rare variant was launched early in 2003. Midlands-based RDS Automotive added six inches (150mm) to the wheelbase of the DB7 to turn it into a genuine four-

Built at Bloxham: the DB7 Vantage Production Line

Building a DB7 Vantage takes a total of eight weeks. Both coupé and Volante body shells are assembled at Mayflower Vehicle Systems in Coventry and delivered to Bloxham painted in grey primer, with corrosion prevention and undersealing already complete. The primer is flatted by hand before the water-based colour coats and solvent-based lacquer are applied in Bloxham's own paint shop, which opened in October 1999. Two technicians paint each car, both of them using paint from the same batch to ensure colour consistency. Each DB7 has a total of seven coats of paint, with a depth of 180 microns.

The first step in the 'assembly' process actually involves disassembly, as the bonnet and boot lid are removed to have their 'hardware' (locks, latches, lights etc) fitted, though the door hardware is fitted with the doors still attached to the car. Then the fuel tank and internal wiring harnesses are fitted from the top while the suspension, rear axle and brakes are fitted underneath.

Two specially trained technicians fit the engine and gearbox, which are supplied as an assembly from Cosworth Technology in Wellingborough. The engine management system ECUs, different for coupé and Volante, Federal and European, automatic and manual transmission are then wired up. The car then reaches its first quality control checks: it must pass these before it can continue to the next assembly station, where the doors, wings, bonnet and front bumper are fitted, followed by sound insulation, carpets and the interior.

Wheels and tyres are fitted next, together with glass and the hood assembly on Volantes. After final interior finishing and checks on steering alignment and safety systems, the cars are subjected to a six-minute water spray to check for leaks. Each DB7 is then road-tested for two hours, including a 150mph (241km/h) run at the Gaydon test track, and any problems rectified. US-market cars are also given a mandatory rolling road check.

After final quality checks, paintwork rectification and a thorough valet, the DB7 is ready for its customer.

Left and above The DB7 line at Bloxham.

seater. Australian company director Peter Malone came up with the idea, which RDS then designed and computer-modelled. The additional metal, which all went into the area behind the B-pillars, was added by Park Sheet Metal in Coventry. The conversion could be applied to any DB7 at a cost of around £75,000. Surprisingly, the extra length did little to compromise the proportions of Ian Callum's original shape.

The DB7 was Aston's saviour at a time when economic conditions were at their worst, and the big V8 models were struggling to find customers. Though some enthusiasts might decry the Jaguar parentage, that's better than no Astons at all – and the DB7 has proved itself to be a very respectable motor car. In its developed form, with the V12 engine, it's every inch what an Aston should be. There's no wonder it's proved to be such a success.

Vanquish, Vantage and the Future

Ford president Jac Nasser owns an Aston Martin DB4, but he wasn't about to let an enthusiasm for Aston history turn Newport Pagnell's products into retro-styled imitations of the past. Instead, he wanted Astons to showcase the latest technology available to Ford – and to become the Ford equivalent of Fiat's Ferrari. So the car that would replace the big V8 Astons was to be more technically sophisticated than anything Newport Pagnell had seen before.

The first signs of what was to come appeared in January 1998, when Aston Martin showed a metallic green concept car called Project Vantage, which made its debut at the New York International Auto Show. At first sight it seemed like a slightly more muscular version of the DB7, both shapes being the work of Ian Callum. Despite the superficial similarities, Project Vantage was a very different car – wider, with a longer wheelbase and different proportions, and fitted with a V12 engine that would not be seen in the DB7 for another year. Project Vantage was constructed in a completely different way to the DB7, too, with an aluminium and carbon-fibre chassis held together with structural adhesives. Like the DB7, Project Vantage's styling received plenty of praise, though it was not without a hint of controversy. Eyebrows were raised at the rather sudden vertical crease in the doors ahead of the rear wheel arches, which served to define and emphasize the shape of the rear end. On the inside, traditionalists noted the complete absence of wood veneer, replaced by polished aluminium and carbon-fibre panels – though much of Project Vantage's interior was, reassuringly, covered in Connolly leather. Speculation that a

Previous page Interior of 1998 Project Vantage.

Below The 1998 Project Vantage concept car.

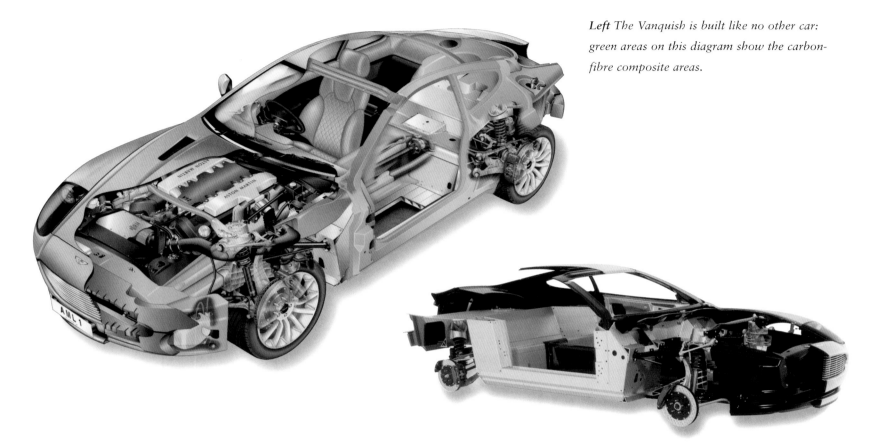

Left The Vanquish is built like no other car: green areas on this diagram show the carbon-fibre composite areas.

Above Vanquish has a strong carbon-fibre transmission tunnel, bonded and riveted to extruded aluminium members.

development of Project Vantage would replace the V8 models was proved correct when Aston Martin announced details of its new flagship model in October 2000. Prediction that it was to be called DB8 or even DB9 was wide of the mark, however: the new car was the V12 Vanquish, and it differed only in detail from Project Vantage.

Such was the response to Project Vantage that a production version was given the green light immediately after the concept's first appearance. Ford ploughed £2.0 million into refurbishing the Newport Pagnell factory in readiness for the new car, which was the subject of the most exhaustive and expensive development programme the company had ever undertaken. A Vanquish body was subjected to temperature extremes of -41°C (-42°F) and +81°C (+178°F) in an 'environmental' facility to prove the durability of the bonded structure. More than a million test miles were covered in 50 prototypes, and sub-assemblies were tested at Ford's engineering centres in the UK, Germany and the United States. Lotus Engineering, the highly respected offshoot of the Norfolk sports car maker, assisted in the new Aston's development.

Like the V8s before it, the Vanquish was to be hand-made at Newport Pagnell, using aluminium alloy body panels. The chassis would be made at Newport Pagnell too, its strong carbon-fibre transmission tunnel bonded and riveted to extruded aluminium members forming the front and rear bulkheads and single-piece composite side panels. The clever composite A-pillars, developed in partnership with Nottingham University, were made from braided carbon fibre around a honeycomb centre. The engine, steering and front suspension were mounted on a subframe constructed from carbon fibre, steel and aluminium, which was bolted to the front bulkhead. Ahead of this sat a deformable composite crash structure which incorporated the traditional Aston Martin grille shape,

Right Like the DB7, the Vanquish was
designed by Ian Callum.

Below Hints of DB4GT Zagato remain.

and provided mountings for the water, transmission oil and air conditioning radiators. A
similar crush zone at the rear was formed by the boot sides and floor, and parcel shelf.
Extruded aluminium beams in the doors provided protection against side impacts. The
underside of the Vanquish was completely flat as far back as the rear axle, where
underbody airflow fed into a venturi shape to encourage high-speed downforce.

The aluminium panels forming the car's skin would be created using a new
'Superforming' process, but they would be finished and fitted by hand. The combination of
traditional craftsmanship and advanced engineering meant that the Vanquish was lighter,
stiffer and stronger than the V8 models it replaced, but retained the build quality for
which Astons were justly renowned. The structure was also said to exceed all known or
planned safety legislation 'by a substantial margin'.

Vanquish V12

The engine that powered the Vanquish was a development of that seen in the DB7 Vantage
a couple of years earlier. In the Vanquish the driver controlled the engine with a 'drive by
wire' throttle pedal: there was no direct mechanical connection to the engine, instead the
pedal position was communicated electronically to the engine management system, which
then selected the appropriate throttle opening. The 60-degree V12 retained the DB7
Vantage capacity of 5935cc (or 5.9 litres, though Aston Martin continue to call it a '6.0-
litre') but it had been treated to a new crankshaft, inlet manifolds, camshafts and valve
gear. The new stainless-steel exhaust system was clad in a heat-resistant material developed
for the aerospace industry. Car magazines initially wondered if the Vanquish might have a
500bhp engine, then reported 450bhp and then 470bhp, but the final power output was
460bhp. That was nearly 10 per cent up on the DB7 Vantage but the Vanquish was also
heavier at 4054lb (1835kg) (compared to 3924lb [1780kg] for the DB7). Even so, Aston
Martin claimed the Vanquish would be comfortably quicker than the previous cars
reaching speeds in excess of 190mph (306km/h) and beating 4.5 seconds for the 0-60mph
(97km/h) benchmark. The Vanquish was said to reach 100mph (161km/h) from rest in less
than 10 seconds, which was pace enough to frighten Ferrari.

Building the Vanquish

No other car in the world is built in quite the same way as the Aston Martin Vanquish. Building a Vanquish combines the latest techniques and technology, developed with Ford Research and Lotus Engineering, with the traditional skills of Newport Pagnell craftsmen.

The car's aluminium panels are created by a new technique called 'Superforming' where sheet aluminium heated to 500°C (932°F) is placed in a mould and compressed air is used to force the aluminium into the desired shape. This technique produces high-quality panels, and when production volumes are low it is also cheaper than conventional press tools. The Superformed inner and outer skins are built up into finished panels using traditional panel-beating skills. The panels are made in the area of the factory where the chassis for the V8 models used to be welded together.

The aluminium and carbon-fibre tub is bonded together in an assembly jig, all based around the carbon-fibre transmission tunnel. Assembly begins with the boot floor and lamp pods, then the special carbon/honeycomb A-posts, the heater plenum chamber and the roof header rail, followed by the rear screen surround, side panels and roof. Two 40-minute breaks in the assembly process allow the adhesives to cure.

Forming panels and assembling the body take about 43 hours, and another 54 hours go into preparing and painting the car by hand, in essentially the same way as the DB7 and the previous V8 range. Final assembly begins with the petrol tank and pipework, then the wiring harnesses and sound insulation.

The brakes and differential are fitted to the rear subframe, while a front 'cradle' is assembled which includes the suspension towers. These are then fitted using another jig, followed by the engine and gearbox and the bonded crash structure which protects occupants in a collision. After fitting the exhaust and making final connections, the engine starts for the first time *in situ*.

The doors are built up as a sub-assembly, then fitted and aligned, followed by the bumpers and the bonnet. Meanwhile, the interior trim is fitted: eight hides are used in every car. After 142 hours of assembly time, the car is ready for testing.

After a water leak check and rolling road test, each Vanquish is tested on the roads around Newport Pagnell and at the nearby Millbrook Proving Ground. After a final quality inspection, the Vanquish is then complete, after a build process taking around 317 hours.

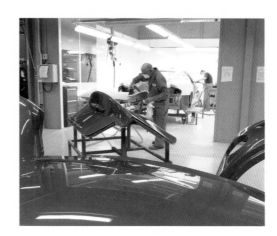

Left Assembling the Vanquish front suspension.
Top Newport Pagnell's paint shop.
Above Traditional skills are still vital.

Above and right The Vanquish V12 engine develops 460bhp.

2001 V12 Vanquish

Engine:	V12, twin-overhead-cam per bank, four valves per cylinder
Bore/stroke:	89mm x 79.5mm
Capacity:	5935cc
Power:	460bhp @ 6500rpm
Fuel system:	Ford Visteon engine management
Gearbox:	6-speed manual transmission with 'paddle shift'
Chassis/body:	Bonded carbon-fibre and aluminium structure with aluminium outer panels
Suspension:	Front: wishbones with coil springs and anti-roll bar. Rear: wishbones with coil springs and anti-roll bar
Brakes:	Cross-drilled ventilated discs all round, with Teves anti-lock
Top speed:	190mph (306km/h)
Acceleration:	0-60mph (97km/h) in 5.0sec

Paddle shift

The traditional gearchange was gone, the driver selecting gears using Formula One-style fingertip 'paddles' behind the steering wheel which operated the close-ratio 6-speed gearbox electro-hydraulically. Developed by Ford and Italian electronics supplier Magneti Marelli, the system could complete gearchanges in less than 250 milliseconds. A fully automatic mode could be engaged for effortless driving, and the transmission also incorporated a winter setting to minimize wheelspin in slippery conditions. Brembo brakes with ventilated, cross-drilled front discs and four-piston calipers were backed by a Teves vacuum-assisted anti-lock system. The suspension had a classical arrangement with double (aluminium) wishbones, coil springs and an anti-roll bar at each end. Bespoke Yokohama tyres with 'AML' moulded into the sidewalls were fitted to 19-inch forged alloy wheels, and had their pressures and temperatures constantly monitored by an onboard system.

Inside, the quality of the trim was not in any doubt – for instance, each interior demanded eight Connolly hides and 129 square feet (12m²) of Wilton carpet. The show car's futuristic interior had been toned down, though high-tech metals instead of wood veneers were still the standard finish. Customers could order a more traditional interior if they wished. Either way the effect was less of a success than the more futuristic interior of the show car, with little of the visual interest of Project Vantage's interior. Unsuitable trim colours could leave the Vanquish cabin looking surprisingly uninteresting. Customers would be invited to Newport Pagnell to select from the limitless range of body and trim colours, and to decide between the two-plus-two configuration and the two-seater layout. Whichever they chose the price was the same: £145,000 ($228,000) is certainly a lot of money, but it seemed remarkable value for such an accomplished car. It meant that the Vanquish entered the market at roughly the same price as the outgoing V8 Coupé, around £40,000 cheaper than the final Le Mans Vantage. Ferrari's only 2+2, the 5.5-litre V12 456, cost significantly more – and wasn't as fast.

The first production Vanquish left Newport Pagnell in September 2001, bound for Hertfordshire and duty as a demonstrator for Aston dealer Grange of Welwyn. Fitted with an array of options including satellite navigation and a premium audio system, the 2+2 Vanquish was finished in a rather insipid (or subtle, depending on your viewpoint) combination of Skye Silver paintwork with grey Connolly leather and grey Wilton carpet. Six months later Ian Minards, Aston Martin's sales manager and previously the Vanquish programme manager, presented a Vanquish to the Heritage Motor Centre for display alongside the Gaydon-based museum's 1934 Ulster.

Gaydon is set to play a much larger role in Aston Martin's future. As well as housing the Heritage Motor Centre and the British Motor Industry Heritage Trust (BMIHT), Gaydon had for many years been the site of a research and development facility operated by the Rover Group. Ford took over the 900-acre (364ha) site from BMW when the German manufacturer sold Rover, by which time the Gaydon site housed a Land Rover test facility. Gaydon was widely tipped to become a new base either for Aston Martin or for Ford's Formula One team, which had recently been rebranded from Stewart to Jaguar. Ford's decision was revealed in 2000 when Aston Martin announced its intention to apply for planning permission to build a new R&D centre and an assembly facility at the Gaydon site. Aston Martin's development engineers, divided between Newport Pagnell, Bloxham and temporary accommodation in Coventry, would all eventually move to the new site.

Above Bespoke Yokohama tyres have Aston logos on the sidewalls.

Below Vanquish interior is less radical than the Project Vantage show car.

Above Ian Minards, the Vanquish programme manager, presents a Vanquish to the Heritage Motor Centre at Gaydon.

Below Aston Martin's new production facility at Gaydon will build a new smaller car, based on this AMV8 Vantage concept.

Taking on Porsche

The impetus behind the decision was the plan to build a third Aston Martin model in addition to the Vanquish and the DB7 Vantage – a smaller, cheaper Aston to compete with Porsches and the more sporting models from Mercedes and BMW. Aston chief executive Dr Ulrich Bez, who had made his name as a project engineer at Porsche, explained that neither of Aston's existing sites could cope with the new model. 'If we are to remain successful, increase sales and generate revenue which will make us self-sufficient it is now crucial that we invest in a third product line,' he told journalists in August 2000. 'We have looked closely at both Newport Pagnell and Bloxham as potential sites for the new model, but recognize that there is not sufficient space at either one of these locations to design, develop and produce an additional model.' Dr Bez also revealed that 'significant increases in production' were planned at both existing factories, following investment in refurbishment and expansion which had exceeded £5 million over the preceding three years.

Development of the new small Aston, codenamed AM305, began immediately and the rumours were that it would be a V8-powered, mid-engined two-seater. A concept car, called AMV8 Vantage, was revealed in January 2003. Ulrich Bez was in no doubt about the car's importance: 'AMV8 Vantage will enable us to appeal to a larger market. Aston Martin will never be a volume car manufacturer, but this model will allow just a few more people to enjoy the Aston Martin experience.' Dr Bez also told reporters that the new car would make Aston Martin 'a true player in the global sports car market'. With total Aston Martin production expected to rise to 4000 cars per year, Aston Martin would be bigger than Ferrari.

Though Ian Callum's three Aston designs (DB7, DB7 Vantage and Vanquish) had been spectacularly successful, Callum was now busy penning new shapes for Jaguar. The new Aston would instead be designed under the eye of Henrik Fisker, Aston Martin's new design director. Fisker had joined Ford from BMW where he had been responsible for the Z8 roadster. 'AMV8 Vantage features many of the design cues that have become the basic DNA for all Aston Martin models,' he says, referring to such features as the grille shape

and wing vents. 'It was important to ensure that the car's design was pure, clean and modern, while at the same time you should be able to put your hand over the front nose badge and still recognize the car as an Aston Martin.' The design brief was to make the new car look purposeful and powerful, but still elegant and classic – Aston Martin described it as a 'muscular athlete wearing a tailor-made suit'.

The bonnet is long, despite the compact V8 engine underneath, because the engine is mounted as far back as possible – just like Touring's DBSC of 1966. This 'front mid-engined' layout improves weight distribution and reduces the car's polar moment of inertia, both of which improve handling. The gearbox is at the back of the car in unit with the rear axle, connected to the engine by a torque tube. This makes it sound like the stillborn 'small Aston' project of the early 1970s. Again this is to improve weight distribution, which is said to be almost exactly 50 per cent front, 50 per cent rear. Short overhangs front and rear and a wide track give AMV8 Vantage an aggressive stance, as well as helping the roadholding and ride quality.

Above *Aston Martin's new Design Director, Henrik Fisker.*

AMV8 Vantage is some 12in (300mm) shorter than the DB7 and Vanquish, though in other dimensions it trades punches with the existing cars. It is wider than the DB7, with a fractionally longer wheelbase, while the Vanquish is wider but not as low-slung. Crucially, AMV8 Vantage is said to weigh 'less than 1500kg' which makes it nearly 660lb (300kg) lighter than the DB7 (the Vanquish is even heavier). That should mean sparkling performance, even with its much smaller and less powerful engine. The new car is the first Aston to be based on the 'VH Platform Strategy' which will underpin all future production Astons. VH stands for 'Vertical/Horizontal', the idea being that the platform is adaptable enough in its design and construction that it can be used for a variety of very different models, with different body styles and engines. Conventionally large manufacturers create a number of different sized platforms and then share them between different brands, the masters of the process being the Volkswagen Audi Group, who build everything from entry-level Skodas to executive Audis on the same platform. But that approach means that no marque has its own individual engineering, The VH strategy is intended to make Astons profitable to build while maintaining Aston's engineering integrity.

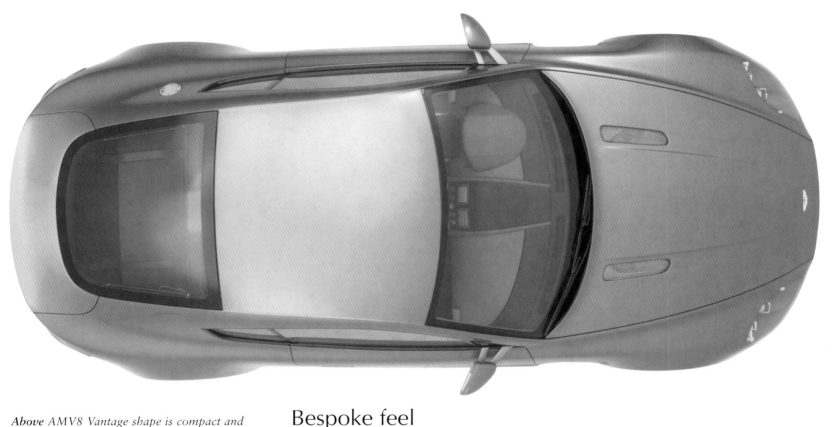

Above AMV8 Vantage shape is compact and attractive.

Below The interior blends traditional leather with modern metal finishes.

Bespoke feel

Aston Martin has given no indication that the AMV8 Vantage concept reveals the final shape of the new car, beyond saying that a key aim in the concept car's construction was that the ideas it embodied could be carried forward to production models. But judging by Aston's previous performance, any changes before production starts are likely to be minor, at least on the surface – both the DB7 and the Vanquish went into production looking almost identical to the show cars that had preceded them.

The concept's interior is much more attractive than the production Vanquish, and again combines traditional leather with modern brushed metal finishes. 'From the outset, the look, feel and functionality of the interior was a key priority,' said Henrik Fisker at the car's announcement. As a result, a lot of effort has gone into developing a cabin with a bespoke feel, following the criticisms levelled at previous Astons for using Ford, Jaguar and Mazda hardware. The AMV8 Vantage uses unique switches and instrumentation said to owe more to high-end watch and hi-fi design than to conventional car interiors. The luggage space is reached using a lift-up tailgate, common enough today but unusual for an Aston – the only previous hatchback Aston Martin was the DB Mark III of 1957.

Few details have been released about the engine, though Aston Martin have confirmed that it will be a V8 unit of 4.3 litres displacement. Almost certainly it will be a 90 degree V8 with twin camshafts per cylinder bank and four valves per cylinder, designed by Aston Martin with help from Ford and probably to be built by Cosworth Technology at Wellingborough. It's not unlikely that the V8 will share some of its components and engineering with the existing V12 – valves, valve springs, tappets and camshafts could all be common, as could the combustion chamber and port designs. The V8 would of course need a new crankshaft, but the connecting rods, pistons and rings could also be V12 components. If that's the case, it suggests that the V8 and V12 have a common bore of

Maintaining Tradition: Works Service at Newport Pagnell

Established in 1964 Newport Pagnell's service department, now known as Works Service, is the biggest and best-equipped Aston and Lagonda service facility in the world. But the Works Service operation goes far beyond mere servicing.

Works Service has its own research and development section, which has produced upgrades for many Aston Martin models including the well-known 6.3-litre conversions for the V8 models and the 'Driving Dynamics' upgrades for the DB7. Astons with 'Works Prepared' badges are serious motor cars. 'Sympathetic' upgrades for earlier models are also available: for instance, Works Service can add modern air conditioning and in-car entertainment equipment to the DB4 while at the same time preserving the car's period feel.

Newport Pagnell also restores and rebuilds classic Aston Martins, retaining the knowledge and the traditional panel-beating and trimming skills that were used to build the cars in the first place. Works Service recently restored a DB6 which was owned by then-Beatle Paul McCartney.

The unique construction of the Vanquish has also given Works Service a new role, as the new car's first designated body-repair facility, operating the special repair and alignment equipment demanded for work on the car's innovative bonded structure. 'The V12 Vanquish is a very special vehicle and therefore needs a specialist approach,' says Kingsley Riding-Felce, Aston Martin's Director of Sales and Restoration. 'We have made investment in tools, measuring equipment, jigs and temperature-controlled bonding rooms to cater for all eventualities.' Three more Vanquish repair facilities are being set up, two in the USA and one in Asia.

Below left Unpainted DB4GT Zagato at Works Service, next to a DB7 with a Vantage behind.
Below Attention for DP114/2 (see Chapter 4).
Bottom The Prince of Wales' V8 Vantage Volante at Works Service.

89mm, which would give the 4.3-litre V8 a stroke of about 86mm. If the V8 matches the Vanquish V12's output per litre then it should develop about 330bhp. At that level neither the V8 nor the V12 is particularly stressed, so more power should be easily available. Dr Bez has been quoted as speculating that a 450bhp V8 might be a possibility at some point.

Right Influences include watch and hi-fi design.

Below AMV8 Vantage is a practical hatchback.

2004 AMV8 Vantage*

Engine:	V8, twin-overhead-cam per bank, four valves per cylinder
Bore/stroke:	89mm x 86mm
Capacity:	4280cc
Power:	315bhp @ 6500rpm
Fuel system:	Ford Visteon engine management
Gearbox:	6-speed manual transmission with 'paddle shift'
Chassis/body:	Bonded carbon-fibre and aluminium structure with aluminium and composite outer panels
Suspension:	Front: wishbones with coil springs and anti-roll bar. Rear: wishbones with coil springs and anti-roll bar
Brakes:	Cross-drilled ventilated discs all round, with Teves anti-lock
Top speed:	170mph (274km/h)
Acceleration:	0-60mph (97km/h) in 5.0sec

* Few official details of AMV8 Vantage had been released at the time of writing, so these specifications are speculative

There has been speculation that the production version of the AMV8 Vantage will be called DB8, though the pundits have been quick to associate that moniker with just about every new Aston since 1993, particularly the V12 DB7 and the Vanquish. All Aston Martin will say is that the Vantage name 'will also be adopted for the production version' and that Vantage is being used as a model name rather than the usual practice of denoting a high performance version, which sounds rather like the six-cylinder Vantage introduced in the Company Developments era. On the other hand, the plan could be to call the new car a DB8 Vantage.

The future for Aston Martin

Whatever it is called, if the AMV8 Vantage project is on time it should debut in production form towards the end of 2004, probably at the Birmingham Motor Show, or possibly at the Geneva Salon early in 2005. A Volante version is almost certain to follow a year or so after the coupé's introduction, with a higher-performance version – perhaps using that 450bhp V8 – following a year or two later. The next production car launch after the AMV8 Vantage will probably be a Vanquish Volante sometime in 2005, and we may also see a 'Vanquish GT' with more power and higher performance than the existing model. If the new 4.3-litre V8 is related to the existing V12, as seems likely, then the V12 may also be able to use that 86mm stroke – which would expand it to 6.4-litres, enough to develop at least 500bhp. And if the V8 is good for 450bhp in modified form, then a 6.4-litre V12 ought to be able to pump out around 670bhp – and that would give the Vanquish GT a top speed well in excess of 200mph (322km/h). But a more important step for Aston Martin will be the replacement of the DB7 – likely to be a DB9 if AMV8 Vantage does receive the 'DB8' tag. This will be the second Aston to use the 'VH' platform introduced with AMV8 Vantage. Expect to see a concept car appear some time in 2005/6, with a production model following a couple of years later.

By then we might see Aston Martin back in motor racing. The word from Newport Pagnell is that they are keen to get back into motor sport, though where and when and in what form is still being discussed. It's unlikely that Ford would want to see Aston Martin in Formula One, where it would compete with the Ford-owned Jaguar team – Aston's

AMR1 effort, remember, fell foul of a clash with Jaguar's own racing programme. Sports car racing is almost certainly the arena where Aston Martin would be seen, partly because it conflicts with no other part of the Ford portfolio and particularly because it fits well with Aston's racing heritage. It would be interesting to see the Vanquish on a race track against the V10-engined Chrysler Vipers in GT racing. Even better would be a purpose-built Le Mans car, perhaps using a modified V12 production engine. It would certainly add to the fascinating variety of machinery that has been seen at La Sarthe over the past few years – Audi, BMW, Bentley and MG have all appeared recently. Building a bespoke sports car would also allow Aston Martin to enter the American Le Mans Series, which would give the brand some useful exposure in the United States, which is a major export market. And why not support each round of the series with a single-model championship for AMV8 Vantages?

Most of this, of course, is pure speculation. But whatever happens, Aston Martin's future looks bright. Soon it will be making more cars of more different types than ever before, and with a level of technical sophistication that is not only several steps beyond the previous generations of Astons but also way ahead of most competitors. Even so, the cars have retained the quality of construction and what Dr Ulrich Bez describes as the 'soul' that make Aston Martins special. The company itself hasn't enjoyed such a high profile since the David Brown period when racing Astons were vying with Ferrari for world championships, and when the road cars were James Bond's latest piece of equipment. Nor has Aston Martin forgotten its heritage: owners of classic Astons are now better served by the factory than for many years, with a new network of 'Heritage Specialists', a parts service and access to build records through the BMIHT. As Aston Martin expands, some chapters of its history inevitably have to come to a close, but at least the will is there to preserve the heritage that makes Astons special. Whatever form future Aston Martins take, it's clear to see that they will have as much soul and character as ever, and they will be as exciting and as fascinating as they have always been.

Below The AMV8 Vantage is the next chapter in Aston Martin's success.

The Name's Martin, Aston Martin

James Bond isn't just the world's most famous secret agent. Ian Fleming's character is also the consummate connoisseur, the epitome of English elegance. Bond is always prepared to perform but never keen to advertise his capabilities. It's no wonder James Bond drives an Aston Martin.

In Ian Fleming's novels, Bond's own car was a Bentley – first a pre-war 4¹/₂-litre with an Amherst-Villiers supercharger, and later a Continental. 007's first use of an Aston appears in the *Goldfinger* book in 1959. Fleming describes how Bond selects a car from the secret service motor pool to track Auric Goldfinger's Rolls-Royce Silver Ghost across Europe. Given the choice of a Jaguar 3.4 or what Fleming calls a 'DB III' (an uncharacteristic factual error on Fleming's part, as the car was really called a DB Mark III) Bond opts for the battleship grey Aston. The car has been specially fitted out with reinforced steel bumpers for ramming other vehicles, concealed storage spaces and a long-barrelled Colt .45 hidden under the driver's seat. Switches can alter the colour and arrangement of the lights so that at night another car can be followed without arousing suspicion, and pursuing cars can be quickly confused. The radio is tuned to receive signals from a homing device. In the book Bond's Aston draws admiring comments from a gendarme in Le Touquet, but by the time Eon Productions came to turn *Goldfinger* into the third James Bond film, in 1964, the DB Mark III was a bit old-fashioned. And the gadgets it concealed were just a little too pedestrian.

Special effects supervisor John Stears and production designer Ken Adam instead wanted something racier, and thoughts first turned to the brutally beautiful DB4GT Zagato. Stears approached Aston Martin, which was initially sceptical – particularly when Stears revealed the modifications that Eon intended to make to the car. Eventually Aston Martin provided two of their latest DB5 models – a production car (originally registered FMP7B) and the prototype DB5, known at the factory as DP216/1, which had started life as a DB4 Vantage. The well-used prototype could be butchered as necessary to incorporate the gadgetry essential to the story, while the pristine production car could be used for close-ups. For filming, both cars used the registration number BMT216A.

Previous page 1965 DB5. This is the second Bond film publicity car, showing some of its special gadgetry.

Right Ian Fleming gave James Bond a vintage 4¹/₂-litre 'Blower' Bentley.

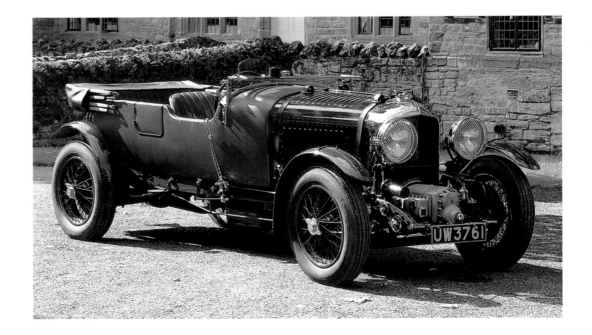

Left Sean Connery poses with one of the two Goldfinger *DB5s in 1964. This is DB216/1. Neither film car had DB5 badges.*

Like the Fleming 'DB III', the DB5 in the film had concealed weapons under its driver's seat, but this time a positive arsenal of them rather than just a single revolver. Instead of the earlier car's reinforced bumpers, on Bond's new Aston the over-riders on the front and rear bumpers extended hydraulically to act as battering rams. The 'homer' from the book was also made more sophisticated. The enemy's position is shown by a light spot on a map, displayed on a screen which was hidden under a dummy radio speaker when not in use. *Goldfinger* director Guy Hamilton was always getting parking tickets in London and wished his car had revolving number plates so he could escape the fines – and so Bond's Aston had three different plates, selectable from inside the car and valid for the UK, France and Switzerland. A mobile phone – almost unheard of in 1964 – was concealed in the driver's door. But that wasn't all.

Below The second DB5 to be built for publicity use after filming was complete. Note the DB5 badge at the bottom of the front wing.

Above One of the DB5 publicity cars, showing the machine guns behind the lights and the extending over-riders.

Right A map for 007's homing device was hidden under a fake radio speaker when not in use.

Tyre slashers, said to have been inspired by the chariot-racing scene in the film *Ben Hur*, extended from the rear wheel hubs. Machine guns were hidden behind the front and rear sidelights. Nails, oil and smoke could be ejected to hamper chasing vehicles, and if the bad guys got too close, an armoured shield could be raised to protect the rear window from gunfire. And the Aston had one more nasty trick: a passenger ejector seat operated by a red button concealed under a flip-up cover on the gear knob. With all the extra equipment the Aston weighed about 300lb (136kg) more than normal, even though bits of bodywork and chassis had been hacked away to make space for some of the mechanisms. Stears and Adam incorporated so much gadgetry into the DB5 that it couldn't all be used in the film. The phone and the battering rams are never featured, and the revolving number plates are demonstrated but never used in anger. Flame throwers and even a cocktail shaker were also part of the original design, but never made it onto the car. Most of the gadgetry worked, at least to some extent – the guns operated, for instance, though they were replicas powered by acetylene gas rather than real, firing machine guns. The ejector seat also worked, if a lightweight dummy was used as a passenger. But the tyre slasher, which Bond uses to stop Tilly Masterson's Ford Mustang (thus introducing the new Mustang to Europe, and replacing the Triumph TR3 she drove in Fleming's book) was built on a separate rig using a mock-up of the Aston's rear quarter.

Bond's Q-car

In the film, the Aston has been prepared by 'Q branch', the equipment and weaponry arm of the secret service. *Goldfinger* is the first film to include the now-traditional scene where Q (then played by Desmond Llewellyn) explains all the equipment to 007 (Sean Connery, in his third Bond film), an idea that came from Bond film producer 'Cubby' Broccoli. Despite playing the ultimate technology boffin for many years, Llewellyn was in reality

Left The DB5's armrest opened to reveal
controls for most of the 'extras'. Again, this is
one of the publicity cars.

hopeless with gadgets. 'Don't ask me about technology,' he once said in an interview. 'I
know nothing about it. I can't work a gadget!' Years later he would be asked to drive the
DB5 in front of a huge audience that included the Queen, and he was worried that if the
now venerable Aston should break down, most of the crowd would expect Q to jump out
and fix it...

The two Astons featured in scenes shot at Stoke Poges Golf Course, in the Furka Pass
in Switzerland, and in Black Park near the Pinewood studio. There the night scenes were
filmed in which Bond, using most of the DB5's gadgets, attempts to evade Goldfinger's
henchmen. Though the two Astons were almost identical, there are differences which are
easy to spot. FMP7B has orange reflectors in front of the air vents in the front wings,
DP216/1 does not. DP216/1 has a chromed trim around the rear number plate which FMP
lacks, and the two cars' February 1965 tax discs are in different positions. Films are often
shot out of sequence, and in *Goldfinger* the result is that Bond often drives away from one
camera in one DB5 and passes the next camera driving a different car. But only the most
dedicated Aston spotters noticed.

The DB5 comes to an inglorious end as it races through a dark factory, pursued by
villains in Mercedes saloons. Bond is confused by headlights coming towards him, which
we later see are his own lights reflected in a mirror at the end of the alleyway. The Aston
crashes into a (fake) wall in avoidance and the unconscious 007 is taken prisoner. Stunt
driver George Leech, whose job it was to crash the Aston, had already put in an
appearance on screen earlier in the film. At the start of the scene in Q's lab he is shot with
a machine gun – and then opens his coat to reveal a bullet-proof vest. The crash seen in
the film was the second take, Leech going straight through the wall and almost out the
other side at the first attempt. The outtake appeared in the trailer for the film that teased
film-goers towards the end of 1964. Both DB5s survived production of the film, more than
can be said of the Lincoln Continental that was one of Goldfinger's limousines. In one of

the film's most memorable sequences the car is crushed at a salvage yard. Ken Adam later revealed that, yes, it had been a real Lincoln.

Making millions

Goldfinger and its four-wheeled star took the public by storm. The film earned back the $3million it had cost to make in just two weeks, making it the fastest-grossing film ever. One of the cars was sent over to New York on the SS *France* to attend the US première in December 1964, and the Aston proved to be a big hit. Corgi's scale model of the car sold far better than anything the toy car company had ever done before, more than two million being sold worldwide – even though they were painted gold rather than silver, for reasons only Corgi knew. For the 30th anniversary of the film in 1994, Corgi released a limited edition of 7500 James Bond DB5 models, plated in 14ct gold. And Corgi's model wasn't the only one. American company Gilbert created a '007 Road Race Set' with a DB5 and a Mustang (blue and red respectively, again different to the colours of the cars in the film) though a manufacturing fault meant that most of the sets didn't work. Two rather more serious scale models, on a rather larger scale, were built by Aston Martin for Prince Andrew and Prince Reza, the son of the Shah of Iran (an Aston enthusiast of many years' standing, who had tried, unsuccessfully, to secure the first production Lagonda). Tadek Marek spent many hours working on these one-third scale 'DB 007 Specials', the first of which was presented to HM The Queen and HRH Prince Philip when they visited the Aston Martin factory a couple of years after *Goldfinger* was filmed.

So popular had the DB5 been that two more replica cars were built for promotional purposes, and it was decided to give the Aston a small role in the pre-title sequence for the next James Bond film, *Thunderball*. After taking to the air using his latest gadget, a Bell jet-pack, Bond lands next to the DB5 and stows the jet-pack in the boot. The Aston is then revealed as having been fitted with some new equipment: rear-facing water cannon to keep pursuers at bay.

***Above** The ⅓-scale model built by Aston Martin for Prince Andrew.*

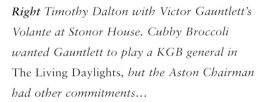

***Right** Timothy Dalton with Victor Gauntlett's Volante at Stonor House. Cubby Broccoli wanted Gauntlett to play a KGB general in* The Living Daylights, *but the Aston Chairman had other commitments…*

That was the last appearance on screen of the original Bond DB5s. DP216/1's story after that reads like something out of one of Fleming's own novels. Aston Martin sold the car a few years later, with many of the gadgets removed and repairs carried out to make the DB5 more drivable and reliable. But once the car's identity became known, new versions of the gadgets were fitted. In this form the car made appearances around the world, and in 1986 it was auctioned by Sotheby's, Florida property developer Anthony Pugliese paying more than $250,000 to secure ownership. Pugliese's collection of 1960s icons also included the gun that Jack Ruby used to shoot Lee Harvey Oswald. In his ownership, DP216/1 continued to tour the world and it appeared in many exhibitions and at museums and events. But in June 1997 thieves cut through the door of the Boca Raton Airport hangar where it was being stored, defeated the alarm system, and made off with what is probably still the most famous car in the world. It has never been seen since. Pugliese's insurance company has reputedly paid out several million dollars on this irreplaceable car.

Bond's next Aston was a DBS, used in the 1969 film *On Her Majesty's Secret Service* which saw George Lazenby take over the role of James Bond from Sean Connery. The Aston's only 'gadget' was a telescopic rifle in the glovebox. Again, two cars were used in filming, even though the car spent much less time on screen than the DB5s had in *Goldfinger*. The DBS is seen briefly at the start of the film and then again at the end, when Bond's new wife Tracy is killed by arch-enemy Blofeld and his henchwoman Irma Bunt.

After *On Her Majesty's Secret Service* 007 would be seen in a variety of cars, most notably the submersible Lotus Esprit in 1976's *The Spy Who Loved Me*, starring Roger Moore as Bond. When Timothy Dalton took over as James Bond after Moore's 12 years in

Above The V8 from The Living Daylights, *showing the skis hidden in the sills and the rocket launchers behind the foglamps.*

Above Pierce Brosnan with BMT214A – two numbers away from Sean Connery's DB5.

the role, the films took on a harder, less frivolous style. To reinforce this idea of Dalton as a more 'traditional' Bond, director John Glen wanted his star behind the wheel of an Aston in the new film, *The Living Daylights*. This time the car was a V8, and it appeared at the film's press conference in Vienna with Dalton and co-star Maryam d'Abo.

More accurately the *The Living Daylights* used two different Aston Martin V8s. The first was a Volante, Aston chairman Victor Gauntlett's own car. This appeared in one of the first scenes to be shot, at the grand setting of Stonor House where Bond is looking after one of the film's central characters, the defector General Koskov. Later Bond drops in at Q's workshop, where we see the Volante being 'winterized' with the addition of a hardtop. In reality the car that appears in later scenes is a V8, but still with the same B549WUU registration number. Special equipment included skis which extended from the car's sills, rockets hidden behind the foglamps, a laser beam mounted in the wheel hubs and a rocket propulsion unit sited behind the rear number plate. Bond was to use all the gadgets in a scene shot on a frozen lake in Austria in January 1987. The driving stunts were choreographed by Remy Julienne, whose team had created the memorable car chase in *The Italian Job* in 1969.

The scene called for Bond to escape from machine-gun-toting Russian soldiers by jumping the Aston over a wooden hut. To make the Aston appear to fly, dummy cars were built and then fired up a ramp using a compressed-air cannon, but the first attempt ended in disaster when the air valves, affected by the cold, opened very slowly causing the car to fly only a few feet. Instead of leaping over the wooden hut, it landed squarely in the middle of it, demolishing the hut completely. Another attempt the following day was far more successful, the dummy Aston soaring over the hut and into the snow beyond. There, in the story, Bond destroys the car using its timed self-destruct mechanism, making it yet another piece of equipment that Q doesn't get back in one piece.

Pierce Brosnan made his debut as Bond in 1995's *GoldenEye*, which saw the 'return' of the best-loved Bond vehicle of all, the DB5. Or did it? Certainly the film was shot using a different DB5, and there was no real pretence that it was the same car, as it was given a different registration number – BMT214A, two numbers away from the original. Was this, perhaps, intended to be another Aston from the same pool as 007's original DB5? Or was this now Bond's own car rather than a 'company' vehicle?

Whatever the car's supposed provenance, the story called for it to race through the mountains above the principality of Monaco, chased by a Ferrari F355 driven by one of the film's villains, Xenia Onatopp (played by Famke Janssen). Again the driving stunts were arranged by Remy Julienne, but during filming of the hectic scene things didn't go entirely to plan. At one point the Ferrari cuts across the inside of a corner to get ahead of the Aston, but when it rejoined the road the two cars collided (director Martin Campbell cuts away just before the collision in the final 'print' of the film). The Ferrari was repaired overnight, and to avoid picking up the bill the producers had to rewrite the scene so that the Italian car won the race. Bond actually gives up the chase when he is asked to stop by Caroline, the young agent who has been sent to evaluate 007 and who is with him, petrified, in the car. The DB5 executes a perfectly-controlled handbrake turn to stop right in front of the camera, and Bond reveals the car's special equipment – a cool-box built into the armrest, containing a bottle of perfectly chilled '88 Bollinger.

Back in an Aston

The DB5 was again seen in the next film *Tomorrow Never Dies*, in scenes filmed in Oxford and in central London. Though the Aston was a welcome link with the history of the Bond films, it played no significant part in the plot. Bond's working vehicles were then provided by BMW, and fans would have to wait until late in 2002 for the chance to see an Aston in another important role, in the latest Bond adventure *Die Another Day*. Predictably, the film's producers and the great and the good at Aston Martin queued up to pay tribute to the Bond film series and its Aston connection on the 40th anniversary of the first film, *Dr No*. 'James Bond and the British Aston Martin car have had a long and successful partnership in our films,' said producers Michael G. Wilson and Barbara Broccoli in a press statement. 'We are delighted to welcome the latest model, the Aston Martin Vanquish, to appear in the 20th film of the series.' MGM's Robert Levin was 'thrilled that Bond fans will get to see James Bond back in the Aston Martin' and Wolfgang Reitzle, chairman of Ford's Premier Automotive Group of which Aston Martin forms a part, said 'When people think of James Bond, the first car they think of is Aston Martin. For all of us that love the 007 films, it is great news that Bond is back driving an Aston Martin, this time our latest and most sophisticated model ever.'

Significantly, Reitzle noted that other Ford vehicles would also play their part in the film. For the first time ever, Aston Martin was involved in a Bond film not just because an Aston was the right car for James Bond to drive, but also because a high-level product placement deal had been done between Eon Productions and Ford – though the word is that Ford paid with technical support rather than up-front cash. The result was that the Vanquish-driving James Bond found himself up against adversaries driving Jaguars (the Coventry luxury car maker being another member of the Ford family). In addition, the lead female character Jinx (played by Halle Berry) drove a new retro-styled Ford Thunderbird. It is a curious irony that Ian Fleming owned two Ford Thunderbirds in the late 1950s and early 1960s, while he was writing the Bond books.

Above Machine guns are hidden under the bonnet vents of 007's Vanquish.

Left Pierce Brosnan with the Vanquish in 2002.

Right 007's Vanquish being pursued by villain Zao's Jaguar XK8.

Above The interior of a special-effects Vanquish, one of four cars modified for use in Die Another Day.

Opposite The grille of the Vanquish opens to reveal heat-seeking missiles and shotguns.

The special equipment that 007 had at his disposal for the latest film far surpassed anything that had gone before. The Vanquish had machine guns that deployed through the bonnet vents, and the grille hid heat-seeking missiles and a pair of shotguns (a curiously 'olde worlde' touch). It even had an ejector seat, an obvious nod to *Goldfinger* in a film which is littered with references to previous films in the Bond canon. Bond is introduced to his new Aston by the new Q, played by John Cleese, in, of all places, a London Underground station.

Aston Martin provided three standard cars to the film makers for close-ups and interior shots. Former Vanquish programme manager Ian Minards and a team of Aston engineers then assisted Eon's Andy Smith and his special-effects team as they turned four more cars – well-used development prototypes – into the highly-modified machines required for the driving stunts and effects sequences. In contrast to DP216/1's appearance in *Goldfinger* 38 years earlier, no single Vanquish was fitted with all the gadgetry.

The special-effects Vanquishes and Jaguars were built specially for one of the film's opening scenes, which takes place on the Vatnajökull glacier in Iceland. 007 is pursued across the ice by his latest adversary Zao in a Jaguar XK8 which sports an unsubtle bodyskirt and an even less subtle machine gun. The film-makers deemed four-wheel drive a necessity on the ice, which meant major modifications to both the Astons and the Jaguars. The engines of both machines were the first casualties, replaced by more compact 5.0-litre Ford V8s. In the Aston this was mounted as far back as was possible in the engine bay to provide space in the nose of the car for weaponry and the driven front axle, which came from a Ford Explorer. The four-wheel-drive systems were tested on tarmac in the UK before filming began, on the assumption that high-grip conditions would be more likely to show up problems. If the modified Astons could survive the test regime, then filming in Iceland would not be a problem. Just in case, the team took a host of spare parts – engines, axles, driveshafts, tyres and more. Nothing broke, though one car slithered on the ice and was damaged, while the script called for another to slide along on its roof. The rest returned pretty much unscathed. 'It has been a lot of hard work, but Andy Smith and his

Aston's Other Roles

James Bond isn't the only screen character to drive an Aston Martin. Over the years, a number of Astons have appeared in films and TV series, many of them playing supporting roles – but some are still well remembered.

Ironically Roger Moore, who never drove an Aston as James Bond, drove a yellow DBS V8 (chassis 5636/R) in the ATV series *The Persuaders*. Except that it wasn't a DBS V8, but a six-cylinder DBS disguised as a V8 with alloy wheels and different badges.

DB2s were the first Astons to appear in films in the 1950s, with a Vantage-engined car in *The Voice of Merrill* and David Brown's own drophead DB2 in *Devil on Horseback*, starring Googie Withers. The 1954 London Motor Show DB2/4 was one of several Astons in the Stanley Baker

racing drama *Checkpoint* in 1956. Another DB2/4 was seen in the Peter Sellers/Lionel Jeffries comedy *Two Way Stretch* in 1960. The same year *School for Scoundrels* went one better, using the ex-Salvadori DB3S/5. A fake tail-fin was added so Terry Thomas could reverse it into a wall and utter a characteristically pithy 'blarst!'.

The two stars of *Two Way Stretch* reappeared in *The Wrong Arm of the Law* in 1963 along with DB4GT chassis 0157/R – until its engine blew up. For the final scenes it was replaced by the works experimental DB4GT, 0167/R. The same year Tippi Hedren drove a DB2/4 in Alfred Hitchcock's *The Birds*. The first time Patrick McGoohan arrived at Port Merion (in the series *Dangerman*) it was at the wheel of an Aston – he would later spend rather more time there in *The Prisoner*.

Michael Caine's transport in *The Italian Job* was a DB4 convertible registered 163ELT. Even though it was a 'preety car', the Mafia still pushed it off a cliff – though in reality a Lancia 'double' made the plunge, not the Aston. A worse fate befell the long-tailed Lola-Aston racer, which was disguised as a Ferrari 512 and then used in a crash scene in the Steve McQueen film *Le Mans*. It was restored by Richard Williams in the 1970s.

Several 1960s Volantes have appeared on screen, one in the Michael Crawford film *Hello Goodbye* in 1970, and in 1985 a DB2/4 was used as a period prop in *Dance With a Stranger*. Most recently, *Tomb Raider* featured a Vanquish, and there's a fleeting glimpse of a DB5 in the Leonardo DiCaprio vehicle *Catch Me If You Can* (2003).

Above Filming Die Another Day: *one of the four-wheel-drive special-effects cars on the Vatnajökull glacier in Iceland.*

Below Filming with the Vanquish inside one of the immense sets.

team have done a fantastic job in creating the special-effects cars,' Minards said at the time. 'We think that Bond's return to Aston Martin will be met with the same enthusiasm and interest as it did back in early 1964 when *Goldfinger* was first released.'

Certainly the return of Aston Martin to the Bond films captured the public's imagination, and there was widespread approval of the Vanquish in its new role. Early in 2003 Bond enthusiasts and Aston Martin buffs started to speculate about a possible return for the marque in *Bond 21*, as the next the James Bond film from the Eon Productions stable will be known until its official title is revealed. As this book goes to press in the summer of 2003, little is yet known about the next production. But Pierce Brosnan will almost certainly return for his fifth (and probably final) outing as 007, and it seems more than likely that he will again be driving an Aston Martin. The word is that Bond's next car will be a much cheaper vehicle that the Vanquish, and that would dovetail neatly with the Aston Martin's plans to introduce a cheaper, third model line – seen in its earliest form in the AMV8 Vantage concept car revealed in January 2003. The release date of the film also fits well with Aston Martin's plans, as both the film and the new car are planned to appear in 2005. Perhaps James Bond, one of Aston's staunchest customers, will become one of the first drivers of the new, small Aston from Gaydon. The details are still to be decided, but one thing is almost certain: James Bond will return – in an Aston Martin.